"After utilizing toolkits from The Art of Service, I was able to identify threats within my organization to which I was completely unaware. Using my team's knowledge as a competitive advantage, we now have superior systems that save time and energy."

"As a new Chief Technology Officer, I was feeling unprepared and inadequate to be successful in my role. I ordered an IT toolkit Sunday night and was prepared Monday morning to shed light on areas of improvement within my organization. I no longer felt overwhelmed and intimidated, I was excited to share what I had learned."

"I used the questionnaires to interview members of my team. I never knew how many insights we could produce collectively with our internal knowledge."

"I usually work until at least 8pm on weeknights. The Art of Service questionnaire saved me so much time and worry that Thursday night I attended my son's soccer game without sacrificing my professional obligations."

"After purchasing The Art of Service toolkit, I was able to identify areas where my company was not in compliance that could have put my job at risk. I looked like a hero when I proactively educated my team on the risks and presented a solid solution."

"I spent months shopping for an external consultant before realizing that The Art of Service would allow my team to consult themselves! Not only did we save time not catching a consultant up to speed, we were able to keep our company information and industry secrets confidential."

"Everyday there are new regulations and processes in my industry. The Art of Service toolkit has kept me ahead by using AI technology to constantly update the toolkits and address emerging needs."

"I customized The Art of Service toolkit to focus specifically on the concerns of my role and industry. I didn't have to waste time with a generic self-help book that wasn't tailored to my exact situation."

"Many of our competitors have asked us about our secret sauce. When I tell them it's the knowledge we have in-house, they never believe me. Little do they know The Art of Service toolkits are working behind the scenes."

"One of my friends hired a consultant who used the knowledge gained working with his company to advise their competitor. Talk about a competitive disadvantage! The Art of Service allowed us to keep our knowledge from walking out the door along with a huge portion of our budget in consulting fees."

"Honestly, I didn't know what I didn't know. Before purchasing The Art of Service, I didn't realize how many areas of my business needed to be refreshed and improved. I am so relieved The Art of Service was there to highlight our blind spots."

"Before The Art of Service, I waited eagerly for consulting company reports to come out each month. These reports kept us up to speed but provided little value because they put our competitors on the same playing field. With The Art of Service, we have uncovered unique insights to drive our business forward."

"Instead of investing extensive resources into an external consultant, we can spend more of our budget towards pursuing our company goals and objectives…while also spending a little more on corporate holiday parties."

"The risk of our competitors getting ahead has been mitigated because The Art of Service has provided us with a 360-degree view of threats within our organization before they even arise."

Collaborative Decision Making
Complete Self-Assessment Guide

Notice of rights

You are licensed to use the Self-Assessment contents in your presentations and materials for internal use and customers without asking us - we are here to help.

All rights reserved for the book itself: this book may not be reproduced or transmitted in any form by any means, electronic, mechanical, photocopying, recording, or otherwise, without the prior written permission of the publisher.

The information in this book is distributed on an "As Is" basis without warranty. While every precaution has been taken in the preparation of the book, neither the author nor the publisher shall have any liability to any person or entity with respect to any loss or damage caused or alleged to be caused directly or indirectly by the instructions contained in this book or by the products described in it.

Trademarks

Many of the designations used by manufacturers and sellers to distinguish their products are claimed as trademarks. Where those designations appear in this book, and the publisher was aware of a trademark claim, the designations appear as requested by the owner of the trademark. All other product names and services identified throughout this book are used in editorial fashion only and for the benefit of such companies with no intention of infringement of the trademark. No such use, or the use of any trade name, is intended to convey endorsement or other affiliation with this book.

Copyright © by The Art of Service
https://theartofservice.com
support@theartofservice.com

Table of Contents

About The Art of Service — 10

Included Resources - how to access — 10
Purpose of this Self-Assessment — 12
How to use the Self-Assessment — 13
Collaborative Decision Making Scorecard Example — 15
Collaborative Decision Making Scorecard — 16

BEGINNING OF THE SELF-ASSESSMENT: — 17
CRITERION #1: RECOGNIZE — 18

CRITERION #2: DEFINE: — 30

CRITERION #3: MEASURE: — 46

CRITERION #4: ANALYZE: — 60

CRITERION #5: IMPROVE: — 76

CRITERION #6: CONTROL: — 93

CRITERION #7: SUSTAIN: — 105
Collaborative Decision Making and Managing Projects, Criteria for Project Managers: — 130
1.0 Initiating Process Group: Collaborative Decision Making — 131

1.1 Project Charter: Collaborative Decision Making — 133

1.2 Stakeholder Register: Collaborative Decision Making — 135

1.3 Stakeholder Analysis Matrix: Collaborative Decision Making — 136

2.0 Planning Process Group: Collaborative Decision Making
138

2.1 Project Management Plan: Collaborative Decision Making
141

2.2 Scope Management Plan: Collaborative Decision Making
143

2.3 Requirements Management Plan: Collaborative Decision Making
145

2.4 Requirements Documentation: Collaborative Decision Making
147

2.5 Requirements Traceability Matrix: Collaborative Decision Making
149

2.6 Project Scope Statement: Collaborative Decision Making
151

2.7 Assumption and Constraint Log: Collaborative Decision Making
153

2.8 Work Breakdown Structure: Collaborative Decision Making
155

2.9 WBS Dictionary: Collaborative Decision Making 157

2.10 Schedule Management Plan: Collaborative Decision Making
160

2.11 Activity List: Collaborative Decision Making 162

2.12 Activity Attributes: Collaborative Decision Making 164

2.13 Milestone List: Collaborative Decision Making 166

2.14 Network Diagram: Collaborative Decision Making   168

2.15 Activity Resource Requirements: Collaborative Decision Making   170

2.16 Resource Breakdown Structure: Collaborative Decision Making   171

2.17 Activity Duration Estimates: Collaborative Decision Making   173

2.18 Duration Estimating Worksheet: Collaborative Decision Making   175

2.19 Project Schedule: Collaborative Decision Making   177

2.20 Cost Management Plan: Collaborative Decision Making   179

2.21 Activity Cost Estimates: Collaborative Decision Making   181

2.22 Cost Estimating Worksheet: Collaborative Decision Making   183

2.23 Cost Baseline: Collaborative Decision Making   185

2.24 Quality Management Plan: Collaborative Decision Making   187

2.25 Quality Metrics: Collaborative Decision Making   189

2.26 Process Improvement Plan: Collaborative Decision Making   191

2.27 Responsibility Assignment Matrix: Collaborative Decision Making   193

2.28 Roles and Responsibilities: Collaborative Decision Making   195

2.29 Human Resource Management Plan: Collaborative Decision Making   197

2.30 Communications Management Plan: Collaborative Decision Making   199

2.31 Risk Management Plan: Collaborative Decision Making   201

2.32 Risk Register: Collaborative Decision Making   203

2.33 Probability and Impact Assessment: Collaborative Decision Making   205

2.34 Probability and Impact Matrix: Collaborative Decision Making   207

2.35 Risk Data Sheet: Collaborative Decision Making   209

2.36 Procurement Management Plan: Collaborative Decision Making   211

2.37 Source Selection Criteria: Collaborative Decision Making   213

2.38 Stakeholder Management Plan: Collaborative Decision Making   215

2.39 Change Management Plan: Collaborative Decision Making   217

3.0 Executing Process Group: Collaborative Decision Making   219

3.1 Team Member Status Report: Collaborative Decision Making　221

3.2 Change Request: Collaborative Decision Making　223

3.3 Change Log: Collaborative Decision Making　225

3.4 Decision Log: Collaborative Decision Making　227

3.5 Quality Audit: Collaborative Decision Making　229

3.6 Team Directory: Collaborative Decision Making　231

3.7 Team Operating Agreement: Collaborative Decision Making　233

3.8 Team Performance Assessment: Collaborative Decision Making　235

3.9 Team Member Performance Assessment: Collaborative Decision Making　237

3.10 Issue Log: Collaborative Decision Making　239

4.0 Monitoring and Controlling Process Group: Collaborative Decision Making　241

4.1 Project Performance Report: Collaborative Decision Making　243

4.2 Variance Analysis: Collaborative Decision Making　245

4.3 Earned Value Status: Collaborative Decision Making　247

4.4 Risk Audit: Collaborative Decision Making　249

4.5 Contractor Status Report: Collaborative Decision Making　251

4.6 Formal Acceptance: Collaborative Decision Making 253

5.0 Closing Process Group: Collaborative Decision Making
255

5.1 Procurement Audit: Collaborative Decision Making 257

5.2 Contract Close-Out: Collaborative Decision Making 259

5.3 Project or Phase Close-Out: Collaborative Decision Making 261

5.4 Lessons Learned: Collaborative Decision Making 263
Index 265

About The Art of Service

The Art of Service, Business Process Architects since 2000, is dedicated to helping stakeholders achieve excellence.

Defining, designing, creating, and implementing a process to solve a stakeholders challenge or meet an objective is the most valuable role… In EVERY group, company, organization and department.

Unless you're talking a one-time, single-use project, there should be a process. Whether that process is managed and implemented by humans, AI, or a combination of the two, it needs to be designed by someone with a complex enough perspective to ask the right questions.

Someone capable of asking the right questions and step back and say, 'What are we really trying to accomplish here? And is there a different way to look at it?'

With The Art of Service's Self-Assessments, we empower people who can do just that — whether their title is marketer, entrepreneur, manager, salesperson, consultant, Business Process Manager, executive assistant, IT Manager, CIO etc... —they are the people who rule the future. They are people who watch the process as it happens, and ask the right questions to make the process work better.

Contact us when you need any support with this Self-Assessment and any help with templates, blue-prints and examples of standard documents you might need:

https://theartofservice.com
support@theartofservice.com

Included Resources - how to access

Included with your purchase of the book is the Collaborative

Decision Making Self-Assessment Spreadsheet Dashboard which contains all questions and Self-Assessment areas and auto-generates insights, graphs, and project RACI planning - all with examples to get you started right away.

How? Simply send an email to
access@theartofservice.com
with this books' title in the subject to get the Collaborative Decision Making Self Assessment Tool right away.

The auto reply will guide you further, you will then receive the following contents with New and Updated specific criteria:

- The latest quick edition of the book in PDF

- The latest complete edition of the book in PDF, which criteria correspond to the criteria in...

- The Self-Assessment Excel Dashboard, and...

- Example pre-filled Self-Assessment Excel Dashboard to get familiar with results generation

- In-depth specific Checklists covering the topic

- Project management checklists and templates to assist with implementation

INCLUDES LIFETIME SELF ASSESSMENT UPDATES

Every self assessment comes with Lifetime Updates and Lifetime Free Updated Books. Lifetime Updates is an industry-first feature which allows you to receive verified self assessment updates, ensuring you always have the most accurate information at your fingertips.

Get it now- you will be glad you did - do it now, before you forget.

Send an email to **access@theartofservice.com** with this books' title in the subject to get the Collaborative Decision Making Self Assessment Tool right away.

Purpose of this Self-Assessment

This Self-Assessment has been developed to improve understanding of the requirements and elements of Collaborative Decision Making, based on best practices and standards in business process architecture, design and quality management.

It is designed to allow for a rapid Self-Assessment to determine how closely existing management practices and procedures correspond to the elements of the Self-Assessment.

The criteria of requirements and elements of Collaborative Decision Making have been rephrased in the format of a Self-Assessment questionnaire, with a seven-criterion scoring system, as explained in this document.

In this format, even with limited background knowledge of Collaborative Decision Making, a manager can quickly review existing operations to determine how they measure up to the standards. This in turn can serve as the starting point of a 'gap analysis' to identify management tools or system elements that might usefully be implemented in the organization to help improve overall performance.

How to use the Self-Assessment

On the following pages are a series of questions to identify to what extent your Collaborative Decision Making initiative is complete in comparison to the requirements set in standards.

To facilitate answering the questions, there is a space in front of each question to enter a score on a scale of '1' to '5'.

> 1 Strongly Disagree
>
> 2 Disagree
>
> 3 Neutral
>
> 4 Agree
>
> 5 Strongly Agree

Read the question and rate it with the following in front of mind:

**'In my belief,
the answer to this question is clearly defined'.**

There are two ways in which you can choose to interpret this statement;
1. how aware are you that the answer to the question is clearly defined
2. for more in-depth analysis you can choose to gather evidence and confirm the answer to the question. This obviously will take more time, most Self-Assessment users opt for the first way to interpret the question and dig deeper later on based on the outcome of the overall Self-Assessment.

A score of '1' would mean that the answer is not clear at all, where a '5' would mean the answer is crystal clear and defined. Leave emtpy when the question is not applicable or you don't want to answer it, you can skip it without affecting your score. Write your score in the space provided.

After you have responded to all the appropriate statements in each section, compute your average score for that section, using the formula provided, and round to the nearest tenth. Then transfer to the corresponding spoke in the Collaborative Decision Making Scorecard on the second next page of the Self-Assessment.

Your completed Collaborative Decision Making Scorecard will give you a clear presentation of which Collaborative Decision Making areas need attention.

Collaborative Decision Making Scorecard Example

Example of how the finalized Scorecard can look like:

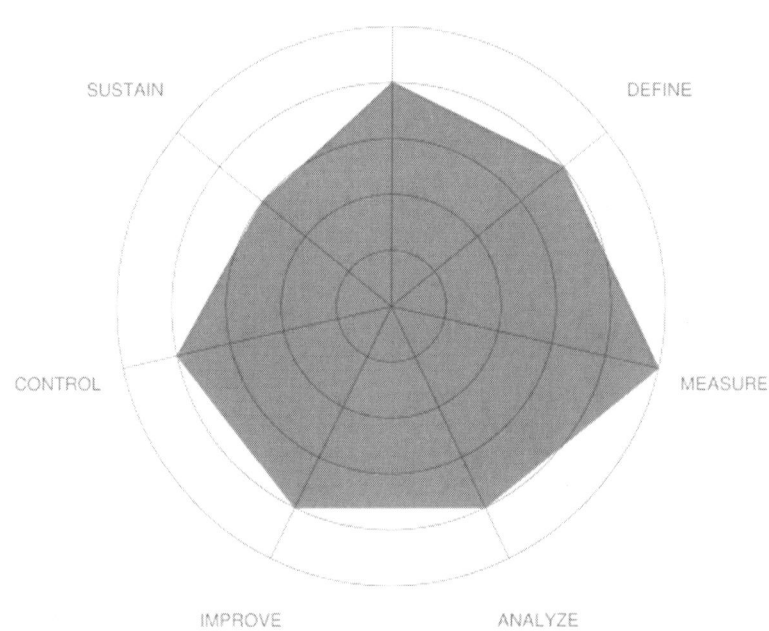

Collaborative Decision Making Scorecard

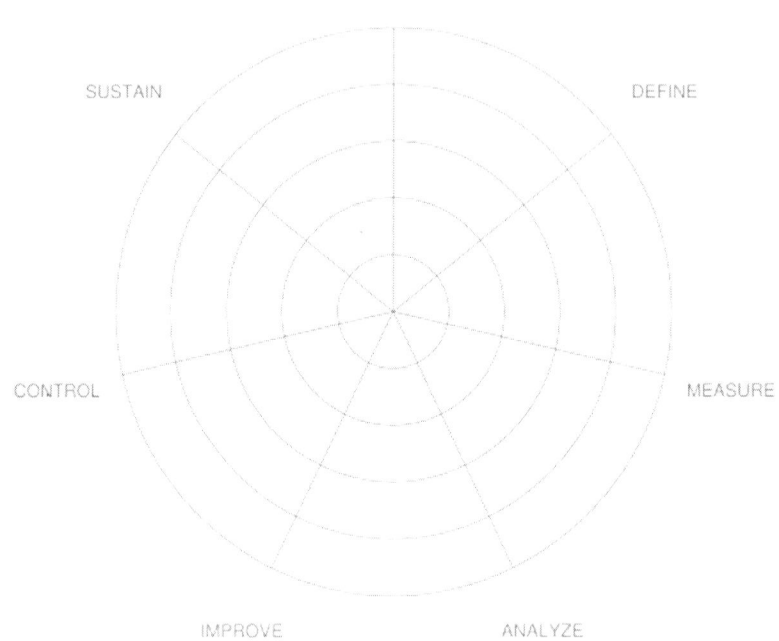

BEGINNING OF THE SELF-ASSESSMENT:

CRITERION #1: RECOGNIZE

INTENT: Be aware of the need for change. Recognize that there is an unfavorable variation, problem or symptom.

In my belief, the answer to this question is clearly defined:

5 Strongly Agree

4 Agree

3 Neutral

2 Disagree

1 Strongly Disagree

1. Are there any revenue recognition issues?
<--- Score

2. What resources or support might you need?
<--- Score

3. What problems are you facing and how do you consider Collaborative Decision Making will circumvent those obstacles?

<--- Score

4. Will a response program recognize when a crisis occurs and provide some level of response?
<--- Score

5. How much are sponsors, customers, partners, stakeholders involved in Collaborative Decision Making? In other words, what are the risks, if Collaborative Decision Making does not deliver successfully?
<--- Score

6. What is the problem or issue?
<--- Score

7. How can auditing be a preventative security measure?
<--- Score

8. How do you assess your Collaborative Decision Making workforce capability and capacity needs, including skills, competencies, and staffing levels?
<--- Score

9. Are there recognized Collaborative Decision Making problems?
<--- Score

10. As a sponsor, customer or management, how important is it to meet goals, objectives?
<--- Score

11. What activities does the governance board need to consider?
<--- Score

12. How do you recognize an Collaborative Decision Making objection?
<--- Score

13. Do you know what you need to know about Collaborative Decision Making?
<--- Score

14. Looking at each person individually – does every one have the qualities which are needed to work in this group?
<--- Score

15. What needs to stay?
<--- Score

16. Who should resolve the Collaborative Decision Making issues?
<--- Score

17. What would happen if Collaborative Decision Making weren't done?
<--- Score

18. Are there Collaborative Decision Making problems defined?
<--- Score

19. What are your needs in relation to Collaborative Decision Making skills, labor, equipment, and markets?
<--- Score

20. Are controls defined to recognize and contain problems?

<--- Score

21. What needs to be done?
<--- Score

22. What does Collaborative Decision Making success mean to the stakeholders?
<--- Score

23. How do you recognize an objection?
<--- Score

24. Are there any specific expectations or concerns about the Collaborative Decision Making team, Collaborative Decision Making itself?
<--- Score

25. What is the problem and/or vulnerability?
<--- Score

26. How are you going to measure success?
<--- Score

27. Which issues are too important to ignore?
<--- Score

28. Which needs are not included or involved?
<--- Score

29. To what extent does each concerned units management team recognize Collaborative Decision Making as an effective investment?
<--- Score

30. Do you need to avoid or amend any Collaborative Decision Making activities?

<--- Score

31. Think about the people you identified for your Collaborative Decision Making project and the project responsibilities you would assign to them, what kind of training do you think they would need to perform these responsibilities effectively?
<--- Score

32. To what extent would your organization benefit from being recognized as a award recipient?
<--- Score

33. Is the need for organizational change recognized?
<--- Score

34. What extra resources will you need?
<--- Score

35. Who else hopes to benefit from it?
<--- Score

36. What is the extent or complexity of the Collaborative Decision Making problem?
<--- Score

37. What Collaborative Decision Making events should you attend?
<--- Score

38. Who are your key stakeholders who need to sign off?
<--- Score

39. How are the Collaborative Decision Making's objectives aligned to the group's overall stakeholder

strategy?
<--- Score

40. How many trainings, in total, are needed?
<--- Score

41. Will new equipment/products be required to facilitate Collaborative Decision Making delivery, for example is new software needed?
<--- Score

42. What else needs to be measured?
<--- Score

43. How do you take a forward-looking perspective in identifying Collaborative Decision Making research related to market response and models?
<--- Score

44. What situation(s) led to this Collaborative Decision Making Self Assessment?
<--- Score

45. What are the timeframes required to resolve each of the issues/problems?
<--- Score

46. For your Collaborative Decision Making project, identify and describe the business environment, is there more than one layer to the business environment?
<--- Score

47. Is it needed?
<--- Score

48. Is the quality assurance team identified?
<--- Score

49. Is it clear when you think of the day ahead of you what activities and tasks you need to complete?
<--- Score

50. Do you recognize Collaborative Decision Making achievements?
<--- Score

51. What is the recognized need?
<--- Score

52. Did you miss any major Collaborative Decision Making issues?
<--- Score

53. What are the minority interests and what amount of minority interests can be recognized?
<--- Score

54. Would you recognize a threat from the inside?
<--- Score

55. What are the expected benefits of Collaborative Decision Making to the stakeholder?
<--- Score

56. Who needs to know?
<--- Score

57. Who defines the rules in relation to any given issue?
<--- Score

58. Are losses recognized in a timely manner?
<--- Score

59. Why is this needed?
<--- Score

60. Can management personnel recognize the monetary benefit of Collaborative Decision Making?
<--- Score

61. Do you have/need 24-hour access to key personnel?
<--- Score

62. What should be considered when identifying available resources, constraints, and deadlines?
<--- Score

63. Are problem definition and motivation clearly presented?
<--- Score

64. Do you need different information or graphics?
<--- Score

65. What are the clients issues and concerns?
<--- Score

66. What do employees need in the short term?
<--- Score

67. How does it fit into your organizational needs and tasks?
<--- Score

68. Why the need?

<--- Score

69. What information do users need?
<--- Score

70. Who needs budgets?
<--- Score

71. Which information does the Collaborative Decision Making business case need to include?
<--- Score

72. What Collaborative Decision Making problem should be solved?
<--- Score

73. Does the problem have ethical dimensions?
<--- Score

74. Who needs what information?
<--- Score

75. What creative shifts do you need to take?
<--- Score

76. Who needs to know about Collaborative Decision Making?
<--- Score

77. What vendors make products that address the Collaborative Decision Making needs?
<--- Score

78. Are employees recognized for desired behaviors?
<--- Score

79. Are your goals realistic? Do you need to redefine your problem? Perhaps the problem has changed or maybe you have reached your goal and need to set a new one?
<--- Score

80. How do you identify the kinds of information that you will need?
<--- Score

81. What tools and technologies are needed for a custom Collaborative Decision Making project?
<--- Score

82. When a Collaborative Decision Making manager recognizes a problem, what options are available?
<--- Score

83. How do you identify subcontractor relationships?
<--- Score

84. What is the Collaborative Decision Making problem definition? What do you need to resolve?
<--- Score

85. Have you identified your Collaborative Decision Making key performance indicators?
<--- Score

86. What is the smallest subset of the problem you can usefully solve?
<--- Score

87. Does your organization need more Collaborative Decision Making education?
<--- Score

88. Where is training needed?
<--- Score

89. Are employees recognized or rewarded for performance that demonstrates the highest levels of integrity?
<--- Score

90. Consider your own Collaborative Decision Making project, what types of organizational problems do you think might be causing or affecting your problem, based on the work done so far?
<--- Score

91. What training and capacity building actions are needed to implement proposed reforms?
<--- Score

92. Whom do you really need or want to serve?
<--- Score

93. Will it solve real problems?
<--- Score

94. Are there regulatory / compliance issues?
<--- Score

95. What are the stakeholder objectives to be achieved with Collaborative Decision Making?
<--- Score

Add up total points for this section:
_____ = Total points for this section

Divided by: _____ (number of

statements answered) = _____
Average score for this section

Transfer your score to the Collaborative Decision Making Index at the beginning of the Self-Assessment.

CRITERION #2: DEFINE:

INTENT: Formulate the stakeholder problem. Define the problem, needs and objectives.

In my belief, the answer to this question is clearly defined:

5 Strongly Agree

4 Agree

3 Neutral

2 Disagree

1 Strongly Disagree

1. Are the Collaborative Decision Making requirements testable?
<--- Score

2. Has a high-level 'as is' process map been completed, verified and validated?
<--- Score

3. Why are you doing Collaborative Decision Making

and what is the scope?
<--- Score

4. Are the Collaborative Decision Making requirements complete?
<--- Score

5. What are the Collaborative Decision Making use cases?
<--- Score

6. Have all basic functions of Collaborative Decision Making been defined?
<--- Score

7. Is special Collaborative Decision Making user knowledge required?
<--- Score

8. What was the context?
<--- Score

9. What is the scope of the Collaborative Decision Making effort?
<--- Score

10. Where can you gather more information?
<--- Score

11. How do you manage scope?
<--- Score

12. Who are the Collaborative Decision Making improvement team members, including Management Leads and Coaches?
<--- Score

13. How did the Collaborative Decision Making manager receive input to the development of a Collaborative Decision Making improvement plan and the estimated completion dates/times of each activity?
<--- Score

14. Are resources adequate for the scope?
<--- Score

15. What happens if Collaborative Decision Making's scope changes?
<--- Score

16. How do you keep key subject matter experts in the loop?
<--- Score

17. Do the problem and goal statements meet the SMART criteria (specific, measurable, attainable, relevant, and time-bound)?
<--- Score

18. Has your scope been defined?
<--- Score

19. Is the current 'as is' process being followed? If not, what are the discrepancies?
<--- Score

20. Is there a critical path to deliver Collaborative Decision Making results?
<--- Score

21. What are the tasks and definitions?

<--- Score

22. If substitutes have been appointed, have they been briefed on the Collaborative Decision Making goals and received regular communications as to the progress to date?
<--- Score

23. When is the estimated completion date?
<--- Score

24. What are the compelling stakeholder reasons for embarking on Collaborative Decision Making?
<--- Score

25. What are the record-keeping requirements of Collaborative Decision Making activities?
<--- Score

26. Are all requirements met?
<--- Score

27. What customer feedback methods were used to solicit their input?
<--- Score

28. What is the scope of Collaborative Decision Making?
<--- Score

29. What critical content must be communicated – who, what, when, where, and how?
<--- Score

30. What are (control) requirements for Collaborative Decision Making Information?

<--- Score

31. How do you gather requirements?
<--- Score

32. What are the core elements of the Collaborative Decision Making business case?
<--- Score

33. Will a Collaborative Decision Making production readiness review be required?
<--- Score

34. How do you manage unclear Collaborative Decision Making requirements?
<--- Score

35. What key stakeholder process output measure(s) does Collaborative Decision Making leverage and how?
<--- Score

36. Have the customer needs been translated into specific, measurable requirements? How?
<--- Score

37. Has a team charter been developed and communicated?
<--- Score

38. What are the rough order estimates on cost savings/opportunities that Collaborative Decision Making brings?
<--- Score

39. What sources do you use to gather information for

a Collaborative Decision Making study?
<--- Score

40. Is there a Collaborative Decision Making management charter, including stakeholder case, problem and goal statements, scope, milestones, roles and responsibilities, communication plan?
<--- Score

41. How can the value of Collaborative Decision Making be defined?
<--- Score

42. When is/was the Collaborative Decision Making start date?
<--- Score

43. What are the Roles and Responsibilities for each team member and its leadership? Where is this documented?
<--- Score

44. What information should you gather?
<--- Score

45. The political context: who holds power?
<--- Score

46. Is data collected and displayed to better understand customer(s) critical needs and requirements.
<--- Score

47. Is Collaborative Decision Making currently on schedule according to the plan?
<--- Score

48. What are the dynamics of the communication plan?
<--- Score

49. What knowledge or experience is required?
<--- Score

50. What sort of initial information to gather?
<--- Score

51. What is the worst case scenario?
<--- Score

52. How will variation in the actual durations of each activity be dealt with to ensure that the expected Collaborative Decision Making results are met?
<--- Score

53. Is Collaborative Decision Making required?
<--- Score

54. What are the boundaries of the scope? What is in bounds and what is not? What is the start point? What is the stop point?
<--- Score

55. Who approved the Collaborative Decision Making scope?
<--- Score

56. What are the Collaborative Decision Making tasks and definitions?
<--- Score

57. How often are the team meetings?

<--- Score

58. Are approval levels defined for contracts and supplements to contracts?
<--- Score

59. Are there any constraints known that bear on the ability to perform Collaborative Decision Making work? How is the team addressing them?
<--- Score

60. How do you think the partners involved in Collaborative Decision Making would have defined success?
<--- Score

61. Is the work to date meeting requirements?
<--- Score

62. How does the Collaborative Decision Making manager ensure against scope creep?
<--- Score

63. Have all of the relationships been defined properly?
<--- Score

64. Are customer(s) identified and segmented according to their different needs and requirements?
<--- Score

65. Are different versions of process maps needed to account for the different types of inputs?
<--- Score

66. Who defines (or who defined) the rules and roles?

<--- Score

67. Has/have the customer(s) been identified?
<--- Score

68. Is there a completed SIPOC representation, describing the Suppliers, Inputs, Process, Outputs, and Customers?
<--- Score

69. What Collaborative Decision Making services do you require?
<--- Score

70. What Collaborative Decision Making requirements should be gathered?
<--- Score

71. Is the improvement team aware of the different versions of a process: what they think it is vs. what it actually is vs. what it should be vs. what it could be?
<--- Score

72. Are accountability and ownership for Collaborative Decision Making clearly defined?
<--- Score

73. How do you gather Collaborative Decision Making requirements?
<--- Score

74. Do you have a Collaborative Decision Making success story or case study ready to tell and share?
<--- Score

75. Does the team have regular meetings?

<--- Score

76. Are required metrics defined, what are they?
<--- Score

77. What information do you gather?
<--- Score

78. Scope of sensitive information?
<--- Score

79. Has the Collaborative Decision Making work been fairly and/or equitably divided and delegated among team members who are qualified and capable to perform the work? Has everyone contributed?
<--- Score

80. Has the improvement team collected the 'voice of the customer' (obtained feedback – qualitative and quantitative)?
<--- Score

81. What is the scope of the Collaborative Decision Making work?
<--- Score

82. What would be the goal or target for a Collaborative Decision Making's improvement team?
<--- Score

83. How was the 'as is' process map developed, reviewed, verified and validated?
<--- Score

84. Are there different segments of customers?
<--- Score

85. Who is gathering Collaborative Decision Making information?
<--- Score

86. Is the Collaborative Decision Making scope manageable?
<--- Score

87. Has everyone on the team, including the team leaders, been properly trained?
<--- Score

88. Do you all define Collaborative Decision Making in the same way?
<--- Score

89. Is there any additional Collaborative Decision Making definition of success?
<--- Score

90. Is the Collaborative Decision Making scope complete and appropriately sized?
<--- Score

91. Is there a clear Collaborative Decision Making case definition?
<--- Score

92. What is in the scope and what is not in scope?
<--- Score

93. How do you hand over Collaborative Decision Making context?
<--- Score

94. What are the requirements for audit information?
<--- Score

95. How have you defined all Collaborative Decision Making requirements first?
<--- Score

96. What intelligence can you gather?
<--- Score

97. Has anyone else (internal or external to the group) attempted to solve this problem or a similar one before? If so, what knowledge can be leveraged from these previous efforts?
<--- Score

98. Is scope creep really all bad news?
<--- Score

99. What is a worst-case scenario for losses?
<--- Score

100. What constraints exist that might impact the team?
<--- Score

101. What is the definition of success?
<--- Score

102. How would you define Collaborative Decision Making leadership?
<--- Score

103. Is there a completed, verified, and validated high-level 'as is' (not 'should be' or 'could be') stakeholder process map?

<--- Score

104. Is Collaborative Decision Making linked to key stakeholder goals and objectives?
<--- Score

105. In what way can you redefine the criteria of choice clients have in your category in your favor?
<--- Score

106. How are consistent Collaborative Decision Making definitions important?
<--- Score

107. What is the definition of Collaborative Decision Making excellence?
<--- Score

108. Are roles and responsibilities formally defined?
<--- Score

109. What gets examined?
<--- Score

110. Have specific policy objectives been defined?
<--- Score

111. Is the scope of Collaborative Decision Making defined?
<--- Score

112. Is it clearly defined in and to your organization what you do?
<--- Score

113. What is out-of-scope initially?

<--- Score

114. What specifically is the problem? Where does it occur? When does it occur? What is its extent?
<--- Score

115. Are audit criteria, scope, frequency and methods defined?
<--- Score

116. How do you gather the stories?
<--- Score

117. What system do you use for gathering Collaborative Decision Making information?
<--- Score

118. How will the Collaborative Decision Making team and the group measure complete success of Collaborative Decision Making?
<--- Score

119. How and when will the baselines be defined?
<--- Score

120. Is the team adequately staffed with the desired cross-functionality? If not, what additional resources are available to the team?
<--- Score

121. How do you catch Collaborative Decision Making definition inconsistencies?
<--- Score

122. When are meeting minutes sent out? Who is on the distribution list?

<--- Score

123. Has the direction changed at all during the course of Collaborative Decision Making? If so, when did it change and why?
<--- Score

124. Is there regularly 100% attendance at the team meetings? If not, have appointed substitutes attended to preserve cross-functionality and full representation?
<--- Score

125. What is in scope?
<--- Score

126. How is the team tracking and documenting its work?
<--- Score

127. How would you define the culture at your organization, how susceptible is it to Collaborative Decision Making changes?
<--- Score

128. Has a project plan, Gantt chart, or similar been developed/completed?
<--- Score

129. What defines best in class?
<--- Score

Add up total points for this section:
_____ = Total points for this section

Divided by: _____ (number of

statements answered) = _____
Average score for this section

Transfer your score to the Collaborative Decision Making Index at the beginning of the Self-Assessment.

CRITERION #3: MEASURE:

INTENT: Gather the correct data. Measure the current performance and evolution of the situation.

In my belief, the answer to this question is clearly defined:

5 Strongly Agree

4 Agree

3 Neutral

2 Disagree

1 Strongly Disagree

1. Are you able to realize any cost savings?
<--- Score

2. What are the costs of reform?
<--- Score

3. Does management have the right priorities among projects?
<--- Score

4. Where is it measured?
<--- Score

5. What is an unallowable cost?
<--- Score

6. How will success or failure be measured?
<--- Score

7. Are there measurements based on task performance?
<--- Score

8. What measurements are being captured?
<--- Score

9. What causes innovation to fail or succeed in your organization?
<--- Score

10. At what cost?
<--- Score

11. Are actual costs in line with budgeted costs?
<--- Score

12. How to cause the change?
<--- Score

13. Was a business case (cost/benefit) developed?
<--- Score

14. Have you included everything in your Collaborative Decision Making cost models?
<--- Score

15. How long to keep data and how to manage retention costs?
<--- Score

16. What evidence is there and what is measured?
<--- Score

17. Is there an opportunity to verify requirements?
<--- Score

18. How will costs be allocated?
<--- Score

19. Which Collaborative Decision Making impacts are significant?
<--- Score

20. How will your organization measure success?
<--- Score

21. What are the operational costs after Collaborative Decision Making deployment?
<--- Score

22. Are you aware of what could cause a problem?
<--- Score

23. What users will be impacted?
<--- Score

24. How can you reduce costs?
<--- Score

25. What is the root cause(s) of the problem?
<--- Score

26. Is it possible to estimate the impact of unanticipated complexity such as wrong or failed assumptions, feedback, etcetera on proposed reforms?
<--- Score

27. Are the measurements objective?
<--- Score

28. What is your decision requirements diagram?
<--- Score

29. What details are required of the Collaborative Decision Making cost structure?
<--- Score

30. How will you measure your Collaborative Decision Making effectiveness?
<--- Score

31. What do people want to verify?
<--- Score

32. What is the total fixed cost?
<--- Score

33. What relevant entities could be measured?
<--- Score

34. How is the value delivered by Collaborative Decision Making being measured?
<--- Score

35. What can be used to verify compliance?
<--- Score

36. How do you measure success?
<--- Score

37. How are measurements made?
<--- Score

38. How do you verify the authenticity of the data and information used?
<--- Score

39. What is the total cost related to deploying Collaborative Decision Making, including any consulting or professional services?
<--- Score

40. Are the Collaborative Decision Making benefits worth its costs?
<--- Score

41. Which measures and indicators matter?
<--- Score

42. What could cause you to change course?
<--- Score

43. What does your operating model cost?
<--- Score

44. Did you tackle the cause or the symptom?
<--- Score

45. How is progress measured?
<--- Score

46. What harm might be caused?

<--- Score

47. What are allowable costs?
<--- Score

48. What are your primary costs, revenues, assets?
<--- Score

49. How can you manage cost down?
<--- Score

50. Are supply costs steady or fluctuating?
<--- Score

51. How much does it cost?
<--- Score

52. When are costs are incurred?
<--- Score

53. What methods are feasible and acceptable to estimate the impact of reforms?
<--- Score

54. How will effects be measured?
<--- Score

55. Does the Collaborative Decision Making task fit the client's priorities?
<--- Score

56. What causes extra work or rework?
<--- Score

57. Has a cost center been established?
<--- Score

58. How sensitive must the Collaborative Decision Making strategy be to cost?
<--- Score

59. What are hidden Collaborative Decision Making quality costs?
<--- Score

60. When should you bother with diagrams?
<--- Score

61. Does a Collaborative Decision Making quantification method exist?
<--- Score

62. What potential environmental factors impact the Collaborative Decision Making effort?
<--- Score

63. What does a Test Case verify?
<--- Score

64. What tests verify requirements?
<--- Score

65. What disadvantage does this cause for the user?
<--- Score

66. What could cause delays in the schedule?
<--- Score

67. What happens if cost savings do not materialize?
<--- Score

68. How can a Collaborative Decision Making test

verify your ideas or assumptions?
<--- Score

69. Are missed Collaborative Decision Making opportunities costing your organization money?
<--- Score

70. What measurements are possible, practicable and meaningful?
<--- Score

71. Are there any easy-to-implement alternatives to Collaborative Decision Making? Sometimes other solutions are available that do not require the cost implications of a full-blown project?
<--- Score

72. What would it cost to replace your technology?
<--- Score

73. What drives O&M cost?
<--- Score

74. What are the Collaborative Decision Making key cost drivers?
<--- Score

75. How do you control the overall costs of your work processes?
<--- Score

76. How do you measure variability?
<--- Score

77. What are the types and number of measures to use?

<--- Score

78. What is your Collaborative Decision Making quality cost segregation study?
<--- Score

79. How do you verify and validate the Collaborative Decision Making data?
<--- Score

80. Who should receive measurement reports?
<--- Score

81. Do you have an issue in getting priority?
<--- Score

82. How frequently do you track Collaborative Decision Making measures?
<--- Score

83. What are the costs?
<--- Score

84. What are the uncertainties surrounding estimates of impact?
<--- Score

85. How do you verify the Collaborative Decision Making requirements quality?
<--- Score

86. How do you prevent mis-estimating cost?
<--- Score

87. Where can you go to verify the info?
<--- Score

88. Are there competing Collaborative Decision Making priorities?
<--- Score

89. How do you verify and develop ideas and innovations?
<--- Score

90. Will Collaborative Decision Making have an impact on current business continuity, disaster recovery processes and/or infrastructure?
<--- Score

91. What are the current costs of the Collaborative Decision Making process?
<--- Score

92. How can you measure Collaborative Decision Making in a systematic way?
<--- Score

93. How do you verify your resources?
<--- Score

94. How will measures be used to manage and adapt?
<--- Score

95. Have you made assumptions about the shape of the future, particularly its impact on your customers and competitors?
<--- Score

96. Are you taking your company in the direction of better and revenue or cheaper and cost?
<--- Score

97. Do you have a flow diagram of what happens?
<--- Score

98. What do you measure and why?
<--- Score

99. What is the Collaborative Decision Making business impact?
<--- Score

100. How do you verify if Collaborative Decision Making is built right?
<--- Score

101. Why do you expend time and effort to implement measurement, for whom?
<--- Score

102. What are the Collaborative Decision Making investment costs?
<--- Score

103. What are the costs of delaying Collaborative Decision Making action?
<--- Score

104. Are the units of measure consistent?
<--- Score

105. How do your measurements capture actionable Collaborative Decision Making information for use in exceeding your customers expectations and securing your customers engagement?
<--- Score

106. When a disaster occurs, who gets priority?
<--- Score

107. How do you measure efficient delivery of Collaborative Decision Making services?
<--- Score

108. How is performance measured?
<--- Score

109. Who pays the cost?
<--- Score

110. Do you verify that corrective actions were taken?
<--- Score

111. What is the cost of rework?
<--- Score

112. How can you measure the performance?
<--- Score

113. Do you have any cost Collaborative Decision Making limitation requirements?
<--- Score

114. Do you aggressively reward and promote the people who have the biggest impact on creating excellent Collaborative Decision Making services/products?
<--- Score

115. Among the Collaborative Decision Making product and service cost to be estimated, which is considered hardest to estimate?
<--- Score

116. What are your key Collaborative Decision Making organizational performance measures, including key short and longer-term financial measures?
<--- Score

117. Have design-to-cost goals been established?
<--- Score

118. Is the cost worth the Collaborative Decision Making effort ?
<--- Score

119. Is the solution cost-effective?
<--- Score

120. Where is the cost?
<--- Score

121. Do you effectively measure and reward individual and team performance?
<--- Score

122. How are costs allocated?
<--- Score

123. Why do the measurements/indicators matter?
<--- Score

124. What are the costs and benefits?
<--- Score

125. What are your customers expectations and measures?
<--- Score

126. What are your operating costs?
<--- Score

127. Are Collaborative Decision Making vulnerabilities categorized and prioritized?
<--- Score

128. How can you reduce the costs of obtaining inputs?
<--- Score

129. Which costs should be taken into account?
<--- Score

130. Do the benefits outweigh the costs?
<--- Score

131. What is measured? Why?
<--- Score

132. How do you aggregate measures across priorities?
<--- Score

Add up total points for this section:
_____ = Total points for this section

Divided by: _____ (number of statements answered) = _____
Average score for this section

Transfer your score to the Collaborative Decision Making Index at the beginning of the Self-Assessment.

CRITERION #4: ANALYZE:

INTENT: Analyze causes, assumptions and hypotheses.

In my belief, the answer to this question is clearly defined:

5 Strongly Agree

4 Agree

3 Neutral

2 Disagree

1 Strongly Disagree

1. How does the technical process support making the decision?
<--- Score

2. Do staff qualifications match your project?
<--- Score

3. Is data and process analysis, root cause analysis and quantifying the gap/opportunity in place?
<--- Score

4. Where is the data coming from to measure compliance?
<--- Score

5. What were the crucial 'moments of truth' on the process map?
<--- Score

6. What do you need to qualify?
<--- Score

7. What are your current levels and trends in key measures or indicators of Collaborative Decision Making product and process performance that are important to and directly serve your customers? How do these results compare with the performance of your competitors and other organizations with similar offerings?
<--- Score

8. How do you feel about collaborative decision making where multiple people are included in the process?
<--- Score

9. What qualifications are needed?
<--- Score

10. What are your key performance measures or indicators and in-process measures for the control and improvement of your Collaborative Decision Making processes?
<--- Score

11. What systems/processes must you excel at?

<--- Score

12. How much data can be collected in the given timeframe?
<--- Score

13. Do quality systems drive continuous improvement?
<--- Score

14. Is the Collaborative Decision Making process severely broken such that a re-design is necessary?
<--- Score

15. Is the gap/opportunity displayed and communicated in financial terms?
<--- Score

16. How do you implement and manage your work processes to ensure that they meet design requirements?
<--- Score

17. Do your contracts/agreements contain data security obligations?
<--- Score

18. What are the best opportunities for value improvement?
<--- Score

19. Can you add value to the current Collaborative Decision Making decision-making process (largely qualitative) by incorporating uncertainty modeling (more quantitative)?
<--- Score

20. What did the team gain from developing a sub-process map?
<--- Score

21. What are the disruptive Collaborative Decision Making technologies that enable your organization to radically change your business processes?
<--- Score

22. What are the revised rough estimates of the financial savings/opportunity for Collaborative Decision Making improvements?
<--- Score

23. What data is gathered?
<--- Score

24. What is the complexity of the output produced?
<--- Score

25. What are evaluation criteria for the output?
<--- Score

26. Is pre-qualification of suppliers carried out?
<--- Score

27. Are Collaborative Decision Making changes recognized early enough to be approved through the regular process?
<--- Score

28. What are your current levels and trends in key Collaborative Decision Making measures or indicators of product and process performance that are important to and directly serve your customers?

<--- Score

29. How is data used for program management and improvement?
<--- Score

30. What qualifications and skills do you need?
<--- Score

31. What internal processes need improvement?
<--- Score

32. How do you identify specific Collaborative Decision Making investment opportunities and emerging trends?
<--- Score

33. What qualifies as competition?
<--- Score

34. What kind of crime could a potential new hire have committed that would not only not disqualify him/her from being hired by your organization, but would actually indicate that he/she might be a particularly good fit?
<--- Score

35. Were any designed experiments used to generate additional insight into the data analysis?
<--- Score

36. Do you understand your management processes today?
<--- Score

37. When should a process be art not science?

<--- Score

38. Is the suppliers process defined and controlled?
<--- Score

39. What process improvements will be needed?
<--- Score

40. What conclusions were drawn from the team's data collection and analysis? How did the team reach these conclusions?
<--- Score

41. Is the performance gap determined?
<--- Score

42. How do you use Collaborative Decision Making data and information to support organizational decision making and innovation?
<--- Score

43. Is there any way to speed up the process?
<--- Score

44. An organizationally feasible system request is one that considers the mission, goals and objectives of the organization, key questions are: is the Collaborative Decision Making solution request practical and will it solve a problem or take advantage of an opportunity to achieve company goals?
<--- Score

45. Were Pareto charts (or similar) used to portray the 'heavy hitters' (or key sources of variation)?
<--- Score

46. Was a cause-and-effect diagram used to explore the different types of causes (or sources of variation)?
<--- Score

47. What are the Collaborative Decision Making design outputs?
<--- Score

48. What are the personnel training and qualifications required?
<--- Score

49. What types of data do your Collaborative Decision Making indicators require?
<--- Score

50. How is the data gathered?
<--- Score

51. What are the processes for audit reporting and management?
<--- Score

52. What successful thing are you doing today that may be blinding you to new growth opportunities?
<--- Score

53. Do your employees have the opportunity to do what they do best everyday?
<--- Score

54. What is the Value Stream Mapping?
<--- Score

55. Which Collaborative Decision Making data should be retained?

<--- Score

56. Are all team members qualified for all tasks?
<--- Score

57. How can risk management be tied procedurally to process elements?
<--- Score

58. How do you ensure that the Collaborative Decision Making opportunity is realistic?
<--- Score

59. How do your work systems and key work processes relate to and capitalize on your core competencies?
<--- Score

60. How many input/output points does it require?
<--- Score

61. What is your organizations system for selecting qualified vendors?
<--- Score

62. What tools were used to narrow the list of possible causes?
<--- Score

63. What are the necessary qualifications?
<--- Score

64. Who will gather what data?
<--- Score

65. Is there an established change management

process?
<--- Score

66. What methods do you use to gather Collaborative Decision Making data?
<--- Score

67. Has data output been validated?
<--- Score

68. Who gets your output?
<--- Score

69. What controls do you have in place to protect data?
<--- Score

70. Identify an operational issue in your organization, for example, could a particular task be done more quickly or more efficiently by Collaborative Decision Making?
<--- Score

71. What will drive Collaborative Decision Making change?
<--- Score

72. How will the data be checked for quality?
<--- Score

73. What, related to, Collaborative Decision Making processes does your organization outsource?
<--- Score

74. What were the financial benefits resulting from any 'ground fruit or low-hanging fruit' (quick fixes)?

<--- Score

75. How will corresponding data be collected?
<--- Score

76. What output to create?
<--- Score

77. What are the processes that enable to go from shared awareness to shared understanding to collaborative decision making?
<--- Score

78. How difficult is it to qualify what Collaborative Decision Making ROI is?
<--- Score

79. How do you define collaboration and team output?
<--- Score

80. What is the cost of poor quality as supported by the team's analysis?
<--- Score

81. What Collaborative Decision Making data will be collected?
<--- Score

82. Do established processes facilitate quick collaborative decision making when needed?
<--- Score

83. What process should you select for improvement?
<--- Score

84. Who owns what data?
<--- Score

85. Think about some of the processes you undertake within your organization, which do you own?
<--- Score

86. Has an output goal been set?
<--- Score

87. Are you missing Collaborative Decision Making opportunities?
<--- Score

88. How do you measure the operational performance of your key work systems and processes, including productivity, cycle time, and other appropriate measures of process effectiveness, efficiency, and innovation?
<--- Score

89. Do you, as a leader, bounce back quickly from setbacks?
<--- Score

90. Who will facilitate the team and process?
<--- Score

91. What resources go in to get the desired output?
<--- Score

92. Where is Collaborative Decision Making data gathered?
<--- Score

93. Record-keeping requirements flow from the

records needed as inputs, outputs, controls and for transformation of a Collaborative Decision Making process, are the records needed as inputs to the Collaborative Decision Making process available?
<--- Score

94. What Collaborative Decision Making data should be collected?
<--- Score

95. What does the data say about the performance of the stakeholder process?
<--- Score

96. What training and qualifications will you need?
<--- Score

97. Where can you get qualified talent today?
<--- Score

98. Is the required Collaborative Decision Making data gathered?
<--- Score

99. What are the steps of the performance improvement process?
<--- Score

100. What tools were used to generate the list of possible causes?
<--- Score

101. What are your outputs?
<--- Score

102. Was a detailed process map created to amplify

critical steps of the 'as is' stakeholder process?
<--- Score

103. How is the Collaborative Decision Making Value Stream Mapping managed?
<--- Score

104. How often will data be collected for measures?
<--- Score

105. What is your organizations process which leads to recognition of value generation?
<--- Score

106. How will the Collaborative Decision Making data be captured?
<--- Score

107. What qualifications are necessary?
<--- Score

108. Think about the functions involved in your Collaborative Decision Making project, what processes flow from these functions?
<--- Score

109. Who is involved in the management review process?
<--- Score

110. What is the oversight process?
<--- Score

111. What other jobs or tasks affect the performance of the steps in the Collaborative Decision Making process?

<--- Score

112. What Collaborative Decision Making data do you gather or use now?
<--- Score

113. What data do you need to collect?
<--- Score

114. What Collaborative Decision Making metrics are outputs of the process?
<--- Score

115. How is Collaborative Decision Making data gathered?
<--- Score

116. Were there any improvement opportunities identified from the process analysis?
<--- Score

117. What qualifications do Collaborative Decision Making leaders need?
<--- Score

118. Who is involved with workflow mapping?
<--- Score

119. How are outputs preserved and protected?
<--- Score

120. How do mission and objectives affect the Collaborative Decision Making processes of your organization?
<--- Score

121. Have you defined which data is gathered how?
<--- Score

122. How does the organization define, manage, and improve its Collaborative Decision Making processes?
<--- Score

123. Should you invest in industry-recognized qualifications?
<--- Score

124. What quality tools were used to get through the analyze phase?
<--- Score

125. What are the Collaborative Decision Making business drivers?
<--- Score

126. What is the output?
<--- Score

127. Do several people in different organizational units assist with the Collaborative Decision Making process?
<--- Score

128. What Collaborative Decision Making data should be managed?
<--- Score

129. What is the Collaborative Decision Making Driver?
<--- Score

130. How do you promote understanding that

opportunity for improvement is not criticism of the status quo, or the people who created the status quo?
<--- Score

131. Is the final output clearly identified?
<--- Score

132. How is the way you as the leader think and process information affecting your organizational culture?
<--- Score

133. How was the detailed process map generated, verified, and validated?
<--- Score

Add up total points for this section:
_____ = Total points for this section

Divided by: _____ (number of statements answered) = _____
Average score for this section

Transfer your score to the Collaborative Decision Making Index at the beginning of the Self-Assessment.

CRITERION #5: IMPROVE:

INTENT: Develop a practical solution. Innovate, establish and test the solution and to measure the results.

In my belief, the answer to this question is clearly defined:

5 Strongly Agree

4 Agree

3 Neutral

2 Disagree

1 Strongly Disagree

1. How do you improve productivity?
<--- Score

2. Is there any other Collaborative Decision Making solution?
<--- Score

3. Will the controls trigger any other risks?
<--- Score

4. How do you develop relationships to facilitate flows of information & collaborative decision making?

<--- Score

5. What is the risk?

<--- Score

6. If you could go back in time five years, what decision would you make differently? What is your best guess as to what decision you're making today you might regret five years from now?

<--- Score

7. Who are the key stakeholders for the Collaborative Decision Making evaluation?

<--- Score

8. Who are the people involved in developing and implementing Collaborative Decision Making?

<--- Score

9. Is the Collaborative Decision Making risk managed?

<--- Score

10. Who are the Collaborative Decision Making decision makers?

<--- Score

11. Are risk management tasks balanced centrally and locally?

<--- Score

12. What alternative responses are available to manage risk?

<--- Score

13. How scalable is your Collaborative Decision Making solution?
<--- Score

14. To what extent does management recognize Collaborative Decision Making as a tool to increase the results?
<--- Score

15. How will you measure the results?
<--- Score

16. How will you recognize and celebrate results?
<--- Score

17. Which Collaborative Decision Making solution is appropriate?
<--- Score

18. Are procedures documented for managing Collaborative Decision Making risks?
<--- Score

19. How can organizations optimize strategic and tactical decisions through collaborative decision making?
<--- Score

20. How will you know that a change is an improvement?
<--- Score

21. What are the expected Collaborative Decision Making results?

<--- Score

22. What improvements have been achieved?
<--- Score

23. At what point will vulnerability assessments be performed once Collaborative Decision Making is put into production (e.g., ongoing Risk Management after implementation)?
<--- Score

24. Risk factors: what are the characteristics of Collaborative Decision Making that make it risky?
<--- Score

25. For decision problems, how do you develop a decision statement?
<--- Score

26. Who will be responsible for making the decisions to include or exclude requested changes once Collaborative Decision Making is underway?
<--- Score

27. Is Collaborative Decision Making documentation maintained?
<--- Score

28. What roles do teamwork and collaborative decision making play?
<--- Score

29. How do you deal with Collaborative Decision Making risk?
<--- Score

30. How do you incorporate key elements in investigatory practices/experiences to deal with the complexity of supporting investigatory teams collaborative decision making activity?

<--- Score

31. How can the phases of Collaborative Decision Making development be identified?

<--- Score

32. Does a good decision guarantee a good outcome?

<--- Score

33. What tools were most useful during the improve phase?

<--- Score

34. What should a proof of concept or pilot accomplish?

<--- Score

35. Who will be using the results of the measurement activities?

<--- Score

36. Do those selected for the Collaborative Decision Making team have a good general understanding of what Collaborative Decision Making is all about?

<--- Score

37. What assumptions are made about the solution and approach?

<--- Score

38. How do the Collaborative Decision Making results compare with the performance of your competitors

and other organizations with similar offerings?
<--- Score

39. What tools were used to tap into the creativity and encourage 'outside the box' thinking?
<--- Score

40. Who manages Collaborative Decision Making risk?
<--- Score

41. How risky is your organization?
<--- Score

42. What area needs the greatest improvement?
<--- Score

43. How is continuous improvement applied to risk management?
<--- Score

44. How will you know when its improved?
<--- Score

45. How do you improve Collaborative Decision Making service perception, and satisfaction?
<--- Score

46. How does your organization evaluate strategic Collaborative Decision Making success?
<--- Score

47. In the past few months, what is the smallest change you have made that has had the biggest positive result? What was it about that small change that produced the large return?
<--- Score

48. What practices helps your organization to develop its capacity to recognize patterns?
<--- Score

49. Do vendor agreements bring new compliance risk ?
<--- Score

50. For estimation problems, how do you develop an estimation statement?
<--- Score

51. Where do the Collaborative Decision Making decisions reside?
<--- Score

52. Are decisions made in a timely manner?
<--- Score

53. Is the Collaborative Decision Making documentation thorough?
<--- Score

54. Who manages supplier risk management in your organization?
<--- Score

55. Do you cover the five essential competencies: Communication, Collaboration,Innovation, Adaptability, and Leadership that improve an organizations ability to leverage the new Collaborative Decision Making in a volatile global economy?
<--- Score

56. What are your current levels and trends in key measures or indicators of workforce and leader development?
<--- Score

57. Have you achieved Collaborative Decision Making improvements?
<--- Score

58. Do you combine technical expertise with business knowledge and Collaborative Decision Making Key topics include lifecycles, development approaches, requirements and how to make a business case?
<--- Score

59. What do you want to improve?
<--- Score

60. Are you assessing Collaborative Decision Making and risk?
<--- Score

61. Does the goal represent a desired result that can be measured?
<--- Score

62. What are the concrete Collaborative Decision Making results?
<--- Score

63. How are policy decisions made and where?
<--- Score

64. What risks do you need to manage?
<--- Score

65. How do you keep improving Collaborative Decision Making?
<--- Score

66. How do you measure progress and evaluate training effectiveness?
<--- Score

67. Is the Collaborative Decision Making solution sustainable?
<--- Score

68. Who do you report Collaborative Decision Making results to?
<--- Score

69. What lessons, if any, from a pilot were incorporated into the design of the full-scale solution?
<--- Score

70. What is collaborative decision making?
<--- Score

71. Which of the recognised risks out of all risks can be most likely transferred?
<--- Score

72. How does the team improve its work?
<--- Score

73. Have you identified breakpoints and/or risk tolerances that will trigger broad consideration of a potential need for intervention or modification of strategy?
<--- Score

74. How can you better manage risk?
<--- Score

75. What Collaborative Decision Making improvements can be made?
<--- Score

76. What agreements do you make using collaborative decision making?
<--- Score

77. Risk events: what are the things that could go wrong?
<--- Score

78. What were the criteria for evaluating a Collaborative Decision Making pilot?
<--- Score

79. How do you improve your likelihood of success ?
<--- Score

80. Risk Identification: What are the possible risk events your organization faces in relation to Collaborative Decision Making?
<--- Score

81. Is there a high likelihood that any recommendations will achieve their intended results?
<--- Score

82. How is knowledge sharing about risk management improved?
<--- Score

83. How do you measure risk?

<--- Score

84. Is the measure of success for Collaborative Decision Making understandable to a variety of people?
<--- Score

85. How do you manage Collaborative Decision Making risk?
<--- Score

86. Are the key business and technology risks being managed?
<--- Score

87. Who controls the risk?
<--- Score

88. What is the role of the decider in collaborative decision making?
<--- Score

89. What can you do to improve?
<--- Score

90. What resources are required for the improvement efforts?
<--- Score

91. Do you need to do a usability evaluation?
<--- Score

92. What strategies for Collaborative Decision Making improvement are successful?
<--- Score

93. Are the most efficient solutions problem-specific?
<--- Score

94. How do you measure improved Collaborative Decision Making service perception, and satisfaction?
<--- Score

95. How do you decide how much to remunerate an employee?
<--- Score

96. What needs improvement? Why?
<--- Score

97. What actually has to improve and by how much?
<--- Score

98. Was a Collaborative Decision Making charter developed?
<--- Score

99. Who controls key decisions that will be made?
<--- Score

100. Do you have the optimal project management team structure?
<--- Score

101. Would you develop a Collaborative Decision Making Communication Strategy?
<--- Score

102. When you map the key players in your own work and the types/domains of relationships with them, which relationships do you find easy and which challenging, and why?

<--- Score

103. Who are the Collaborative Decision Making decision-makers?
<--- Score

104. Is the scope clearly documented?
<--- Score

105. How significant is the improvement in the eyes of the end user?
<--- Score

106. How can you improve performance?
<--- Score

107. What is the magnitude of the improvements?
<--- Score

108. What current systems have to be understood and/or changed?
<--- Score

109. How vital is collaborative decision making in networks?
<--- Score

110. Can you integrate quality management and risk management?
<--- Score

111. How can skill-level changes improve Collaborative Decision Making?
<--- Score

112. Where do you need Collaborative Decision

Making improvement?

<--- Score

113. Are the risks fully understood, reasonable and manageable?

<--- Score

114. What tools were used to evaluate the potential solutions?

<--- Score

115. Can the solution be designed and implemented within an acceptable time period?

<--- Score

116. How do you manage and improve your Collaborative Decision Making work systems to deliver customer value and achieve organizational success and sustainability?

<--- Score

117. How do tools and attitudes affect collaborative decision making?

<--- Score

118. What went well, what should change, what can improve?

<--- Score

119. Are risk triggers captured?

<--- Score

120. What is Collaborative Decision Making risk?

<--- Score

121. What are the affordable Collaborative Decision

Making risks?
<--- Score

122. What are the Collaborative Decision Making security risks?
<--- Score

123. Is the solution technically practical?
<--- Score

124. Who makes the Collaborative Decision Making decisions in your organization?
<--- Score

125. How will you know that you have improved?
<--- Score

126. What to do with the results or outcomes of measurements?
<--- Score

127. Who should make the Collaborative Decision Making decisions?
<--- Score

128. What were the underlying assumptions on the cost-benefit analysis?
<--- Score

129. Is supporting Collaborative Decision Making documentation required?
<--- Score

130. Explorations of the frontiers of Collaborative Decision Making will help you build influence, improve Collaborative Decision Making, optimize

decision making, and sustain change, what is your approach?

<--- Score

131. What are the implications of the one critical Collaborative Decision Making decision 10 minutes, 10 months, and 10 years from now?

<--- Score

132. What are best practices in deploying collaborative decision making and intelligent business operations?

<--- Score

133. How are Collaborative Decision Making risks managed?

<--- Score

134. What is the Collaborative Decision Making's sustainability risk?

<--- Score

135. Collaborative Decision Making risk decisions: whose call Is It?

<--- Score

136. Is any Collaborative Decision Making documentation required?

<--- Score

Add up total points for this section:
_____ = Total points for this section

Divided by: _____ (number of statements answered) = _____ Average score for this section

Transfer your score to the Collaborative Decision Making Index at the beginning of the Self-Assessment.

CRITERION #6: CONTROL:

INTENT: Implement the practical solution. Maintain the performance and correct possible complications.

In my belief, the answer to this question is clearly defined:

5 Strongly Agree

4 Agree

3 Neutral

2 Disagree

1 Strongly Disagree

1. How do your controls stack up?
<--- Score

2. Is there a transfer of ownership and knowledge to process owner and process team tasked with the responsibilities.
<--- Score

3. Does a troubleshooting guide exist or is it needed?

<--- Score

4. Is a response plan in place for when the input, process, or output measures indicate an 'out-of-control' condition?
<--- Score

5. Against what alternative is success being measured?
<--- Score

6. Are documented procedures clear and easy to follow for the operators?
<--- Score

7. Does Collaborative Decision Making appropriately measure and monitor risk?
<--- Score

8. Is there a recommended audit plan for routine surveillance inspections of Collaborative Decision Making's gains?
<--- Score

9. How likely is the current Collaborative Decision Making plan to come in on schedule or on budget?
<--- Score

10. Is there a control plan in place for sustaining improvements (short and long-term)?
<--- Score

11. Who has control over resources?
<--- Score

12. Is knowledge gained on process shared and

institutionalized?
<--- Score

13. Who is going to spread your message?
<--- Score

14. You may have created your quality measures at a time when you lacked resources, technology wasn't up to the required standard, or low service levels were the industry norm. Have those circumstances changed?
<--- Score

15. How widespread is its use?
<--- Score

16. Will your goals reflect your program budget?
<--- Score

17. Has the improved process and its steps been standardized?
<--- Score

18. What are you attempting to measure/monitor?
<--- Score

19. Are you measuring, monitoring and predicting Collaborative Decision Making activities to optimize operations and profitability, and enhancing outcomes?
<--- Score

20. How will the day-to-day responsibilities for monitoring and continual improvement be transferred from the improvement team to the process owner?

<--- Score

21. Is there an action plan in case of emergencies?
<--- Score

22. Is there a standardized process?
<--- Score

23. Can support from partners be adjusted?
<--- Score

24. What are the critical parameters to watch?
<--- Score

25. Will the team be available to assist members in planning investigations?
<--- Score

26. What key inputs and outputs are being measured on an ongoing basis?
<--- Score

27. Who sets the Collaborative Decision Making standards?
<--- Score

28. How will report readings be checked to effectively monitor performance?
<--- Score

29. How do you plan on providing proper recognition and disclosure of supporting companies?
<--- Score

30. What is the recommended frequency of auditing?
<--- Score

31. What are your results for key measures or indicators of the accomplishment of your Collaborative Decision Making strategy and action plans, including building and strengthening core competencies?
<--- Score

32. Is new knowledge gained imbedded in the response plan?
<--- Score

33. How is Collaborative Decision Making project cost planned, managed, monitored?
<--- Score

34. Are controls in place and consistently applied?
<--- Score

35. What is the best design framework for Collaborative Decision Making organization now that, in a post industrial-age if the top-down, command and control model is no longer relevant?
<--- Score

36. How will the process owner verify improvement in present and future sigma levels, process capabilities?
<--- Score

37. What is the standard for acceptable Collaborative Decision Making performance?
<--- Score

38. Is reporting being used or needed?
<--- Score

39. In the case of a Collaborative Decision Making project, the criteria for the audit derive from implementation objectives, an audit of a Collaborative Decision Making project involves assessing whether the recommendations outlined for implementation have been met, can you track that any Collaborative Decision Making project is implemented as planned, and is it working?
<--- Score

40. What do your reports reflect?
<--- Score

41. Will any special training be provided for results interpretation?
<--- Score

42. Is a response plan established and deployed?
<--- Score

43. What is your theory of human motivation, and how does your compensation plan fit with that view?
<--- Score

44. Are the planned controls in place?
<--- Score

45. Are pertinent alerts monitored, analyzed and distributed to appropriate personnel?
<--- Score

46. How do you monitor usage and cost?
<--- Score

47. Are there documented procedures?
<--- Score

48. What are the key elements of your Collaborative Decision Making performance improvement system, including your evaluation, organizational learning, and innovation processes?
<--- Score

49. Implementation Planning: is a pilot needed to test the changes before a full roll out occurs?
<--- Score

50. Is the Collaborative Decision Making test/monitoring cost justified?
<--- Score

51. Does the Collaborative Decision Making performance meet the customer's requirements?
<--- Score

52. What should the next improvement project be that is related to Collaborative Decision Making?
<--- Score

53. What can you control?
<--- Score

54. Are suggested corrective/restorative actions indicated on the response plan for known causes to problems that might surface?
<--- Score

55. Is there documentation that will support the successful operation of the improvement?
<--- Score

56. Is there a Collaborative Decision Making

Communication plan covering who needs to get what information when?
<--- Score

57. Do the viable solutions scale to future needs?
<--- Score

58. Have new or revised work instructions resulted?
<--- Score

59. Are new process steps, standards, and documentation ingrained into normal operations?
<--- Score

60. How might the group capture best practices and lessons learned so as to leverage improvements?
<--- Score

61. How is change control managed?
<--- Score

62. How do controls support value?
<--- Score

63. What is the control/monitoring plan?
<--- Score

64. Can you adapt and adjust to changing Collaborative Decision Making situations?
<--- Score

65. What do you stand for--and what are you against?
<--- Score

66. Are operating procedures consistent?
<--- Score

67. Who controls critical resources?
<--- Score

68. How will new or emerging customer needs/requirements be checked/communicated to orient the process toward meeting the new specifications and continually reducing variation?
<--- Score

69. Does the response plan contain a definite closed loop continual improvement scheme (e.g., plan-do-check-act)?
<--- Score

70. How do you spread information?
<--- Score

71. Does job training on the documented procedures need to be part of the process team's education and training?
<--- Score

72. Act/Adjust: What Do you Need to Do Differently?
<--- Score

73. How can you best use all of your knowledge repositories to enhance learning and sharing?
<--- Score

74. How do you make space for human scale reflection and collaborative decision making?
<--- Score

75. How will the process owner and team be able to hold the gains?

<--- Score

76. What quality tools were useful in the control phase?
<--- Score

77. Is there a documented and implemented monitoring plan?
<--- Score

78. How do you do a better job of planning out into the future?
<--- Score

79. What are customers monitoring?
<--- Score

80. How will Collaborative Decision Making decisions be made and monitored?
<--- Score

81. How do you establish and deploy modified action plans if circumstances require a shift in plans and rapid execution of new plans?
<--- Score

82. Who is the Collaborative Decision Making process owner?
<--- Score

83. What other systems, operations, processes, and infrastructures (hiring practices, staffing, training, incentives/rewards, metrics/dashboards/scorecards, etc.) need updates, additions, changes, or deletions in order to facilitate knowledge transfer and improvements?

<--- Score

84. What Collaborative Decision Making standards are applicable?
<--- Score

85. How do you select, collect, align, and integrate Collaborative Decision Making data and information for tracking daily operations and overall organizational performance, including progress relative to strategic objectives and action plans?
<--- Score

86. Who will be in control?
<--- Score

87. Where do ideas that reach policy makers and planners as proposals for Collaborative Decision Making strengthening and reform actually originate?
<--- Score

88. How will input, process, and output variables be checked to detect for sub-optimal conditions?
<--- Score

89. How do you plan for the cost of succession?
<--- Score

90. What other areas of the group might benefit from the Collaborative Decision Making team's improvements, knowledge, and learning?
<--- Score

91. Has the Collaborative Decision Making value of standards been quantified?
<--- Score

92. How do senior leaders actions reflect a commitment to the organizations Collaborative Decision Making values?
<--- Score

93. Do the Collaborative Decision Making decisions you make today help people and the planet tomorrow?
<--- Score

94. What is your plan to assess your security risks?
<--- Score

95. Will existing staff require re-training, for example, to learn new business processes?
<--- Score

96. What are the performance and scale of the Collaborative Decision Making tools?
<--- Score

97. What do you measure to verify effectiveness gains?
<--- Score

Add up total points for this section:
_____ = Total points for this section

Divided by: _____ (number of statements answered) = _____
Average score for this section

Transfer your score to the Collaborative Decision Making Index at the beginning of the Self-Assessment.

CRITERION #7: SUSTAIN:

INTENT: Retain the benefits.

In my belief, the answer to this question is clearly defined:

5 Strongly Agree

4 Agree

3 Neutral

2 Disagree

1 Strongly Disagree

1. Will it be accepted by users?
<--- Score

2. What are internal and external Collaborative Decision Making relations?
<--- Score

3. Can you do all this work?
<--- Score

4. How do you know if you are successful?

<--- Score

5. Is there a work around that you can use?
<--- Score

6. Which individuals, teams or departments will be involved in Collaborative Decision Making?
<--- Score

7. Why should people listen to you?
<--- Score

8. To whom do you add value?
<--- Score

9. How can you incorporate support to ensure safe and effective use of Collaborative Decision Making into the services that you provide?
<--- Score

10. Is the Collaborative Decision Making organization completing tasks effectively and efficiently?
<--- Score

11. How do customers see your organization?
<--- Score

12. What is the estimated value of the project?
<--- Score

13. Is there any reason to believe the opposite of my current belief?
<--- Score

14. Who do you think the world wants your organization to be?

<--- Score

15. What Collaborative Decision Making modifications can you make work for you?
<--- Score

16. What potential megatrends could make your business model obsolete?
<--- Score

17. Who, on the executive team or the board, has spoken to a customer recently?
<--- Score

18. Who will be responsible for deciding whether Collaborative Decision Making goes ahead or not after the initial investigations?
<--- Score

19. Whose voice (department, ethnic group, women, older workers, etc) might you have missed hearing from in your company, and how might you amplify this voice to create positive momentum for your business?
<--- Score

20. At what moment would you think; Will I get fired?
<--- Score

21. Who is responsible for errors?
<--- Score

22. Are the criteria for selecting recommendations stated?
<--- Score

23. What are the business goals Collaborative Decision Making is aiming to achieve?
<--- Score

24. Who uses your product in ways you never expected?
<--- Score

25. What is your formula for success in Collaborative Decision Making ?
<--- Score

26. Do you have the right people on the bus?
<--- Score

27. Why is it important to have senior management support for a Collaborative Decision Making project?
<--- Score

28. What are strategies for increasing support and reducing opposition?
<--- Score

29. Who is responsible for ensuring appropriate resources (time, people and money) are allocated to Collaborative Decision Making?
<--- Score

30. Who do we want your customers to become?
<--- Score

31. Do you think you know, or do you know you know ?
<--- Score

32. How do you foster the skills, knowledge, talents,

attributes, and characteristics you want to have?
<--- Score

33. How do you make it meaningful in connecting Collaborative Decision Making with what users do day-to-day?
<--- Score

34. Do you feel that more should be done in the Collaborative Decision Making area?
<--- Score

35. Are you maintaining a past–present–future perspective throughout the Collaborative Decision Making discussion?
<--- Score

36. What unique value proposition (UVP) do you offer?
<--- Score

37. Are you making progress, and are you making progress as Collaborative Decision Making leaders?
<--- Score

38. What trophy do you want on your mantle?
<--- Score

39. How much contingency will be available in the budget?
<--- Score

40. Who will provide the final approval of Collaborative Decision Making deliverables?
<--- Score

41. How can you become the company that would

put you out of business?
<--- Score

42. Is the impact that Collaborative Decision Making has shown?
<--- Score

43. Are all key stakeholders present at all Structured Walkthroughs?
<--- Score

44. What is the overall talent health of your organization as a whole at senior levels, and for each organization reporting to a member of the Senior Leadership Team?
<--- Score

45. Why do and why don't your customers like your organization?
<--- Score

46. What do we do when new problems arise?
<--- Score

47. What happens at your organization when people fail?
<--- Score

48. Who is the main stakeholder, with ultimate responsibility for driving Collaborative Decision Making forward?
<--- Score

49. What is the craziest thing you can do?
<--- Score

50. What is the purpose of Collaborative Decision Making in relation to the mission?
<--- Score

51. What does your signature ensure?
<--- Score

52. What management system can you use to leverage the Collaborative Decision Making experience, ideas, and concerns of the people closest to the work to be done?
<--- Score

53. How do you deal with Collaborative Decision Making changes?
<--- Score

54. Are your responses positive or negative?
<--- Score

55. What are current Collaborative Decision Making paradigms?
<--- Score

56. Which functions and people interact with the supplier and or customer?
<--- Score

57. Who will manage the integration of tools?
<--- Score

58. Who are your customers?
<--- Score

59. How do you assess the Collaborative Decision Making pitfalls that are inherent in implementing it?

<--- Score

60. How will you ensure you get what you expected?
<--- Score

61. Do you think Collaborative Decision Making accomplishes the goals you expect it to accomplish?
<--- Score

62. Who will determine interim and final deadlines?
<--- Score

63. Whom among your colleagues do you trust, and for what?
<--- Score

64. How long will it take to change?
<--- Score

65. If you were responsible for initiating and implementing major changes in your organization, what steps might you take to ensure acceptance of those changes?
<--- Score

66. Is Collaborative Decision Making realistic, or are you setting yourself up for failure?
<--- Score

67. Has implementation been effective in reaching specified objectives so far?
<--- Score

68. Who else should you help?
<--- Score

69. Do you know what you are doing? And who do you call if you don't?
<--- Score

70. If you find that you havent accomplished one of the goals for one of the steps of the Collaborative Decision Making strategy, what will you do to fix it?
<--- Score

71. What must you excel at?
<--- Score

72. How do you maintain Collaborative Decision Making's Integrity?
<--- Score

73. How do you manage Collaborative Decision Making Knowledge Management (KM)?
<--- Score

74. What have you done to protect your business from competitive encroachment?
<--- Score

75. What is something you believe that nearly no one agrees with you on?
<--- Score

76. How are you doing compared to your industry?
<--- Score

77. Is a Collaborative Decision Making team work effort in place?
<--- Score

78. Who have you, as a company, historically been

when you've been at your best?
<--- Score

79. What relationships among Collaborative Decision Making trends do you perceive?
<--- Score

80. How do you engage the workforce, in addition to satisfying them?
<--- Score

81. How do you ensure that implementations of Collaborative Decision Making products are done in a way that ensures safety?
<--- Score

82. Are you satisfied with your current role? If not, what is missing from it?
<--- Score

83. What would you recommend your friend do if he/she were facing this dilemma?
<--- Score

84. Who are the key stakeholders?
<--- Score

85. If you had to rebuild your organization without any traditional competitive advantages (i.e., no killer technology, promising research, innovative product/service delivery model, etcetera), how would your people have to approach their work and collaborate together in order to create the necessary conditions for success?
<--- Score

86. How do you lead with Collaborative Decision Making in mind?
<--- Score

87. What is the kind of project structure that would be appropriate for your Collaborative Decision Making project, should it be formal and complex, or can it be less formal and relatively simple?
<--- Score

88. What you are going to do to affect the numbers?
<--- Score

89. What will be the consequences to the stakeholder (financial, reputation etc) if Collaborative Decision Making does not go ahead or fails to deliver the objectives?
<--- Score

90. Where can you break convention?
<--- Score

91. Have new benefits been realized?
<--- Score

92. What projects are going on in the organization today, and what resources are those projects using from the resource pools?
<--- Score

93. What are the barriers to increased Collaborative Decision Making production?
<--- Score

94. What one word do you want to own in the minds of your customers, employees, and partners?

<--- Score

95. How do you track customer value, profitability or financial return, organizational success, and sustainability?
<--- Score

96. How do you proactively clarify deliverables and Collaborative Decision Making quality expectations?
<--- Score

97. Is a Collaborative Decision Making breakthrough on the horizon?
<--- Score

98. How do you go about securing Collaborative Decision Making?
<--- Score

99. Is your strategy driving your strategy? Or is the way in which you allocate resources driving your strategy?
<--- Score

100. What is an unauthorized commitment?
<--- Score

101. Have benefits been optimized with all key stakeholders?
<--- Score

102. What Collaborative Decision Making skills are most important?
<--- Score

103. Do you have past Collaborative Decision Making

successes?

<--- Score

104. What did you miss in the interview for the worst hire you ever made?

<--- Score

105. What knowledge, skills and characteristics mark a good Collaborative Decision Making project manager?

<--- Score

106. Do you know who is a friend or a foe?

<--- Score

107. Which models, tools and techniques are necessary?

<--- Score

108. How will you insure seamless interoperability of Collaborative Decision Making moving forward?

<--- Score

109. What is the source of the strategies for Collaborative Decision Making strengthening and reform?

<--- Score

110. What are the potential basics of Collaborative Decision Making fraud?

<--- Score

111. How does Collaborative Decision Making integrate with other stakeholder initiatives?

<--- Score

112. What are your personal philosophies regarding Collaborative Decision Making and how do they influence your work?
<--- Score

113. What is it like to work for you?
<--- Score

114. Are you changing as fast as the world around you?
<--- Score

115. Were lessons learned captured and communicated?
<--- Score

116. What is your BATNA (best alternative to a negotiated agreement)?
<--- Score

117. What is your competitive advantage?
<--- Score

118. In the past year, what have you done (or could you have done) to increase the accurate perception of your company/brand as ethical and honest?
<--- Score

119. Who are four people whose careers you have enhanced?
<--- Score

120. Which Collaborative Decision Making goals are the most important?
<--- Score

121. What are you trying to prove to yourself, and how might it be hijacking your life and business success?
<--- Score

122. What is the funding source for this project?
<--- Score

123. What counts that you are not counting?
<--- Score

124. What may be the consequences for the performance of an organization if all stakeholders are not consulted regarding Collaborative Decision Making?
<--- Score

125. What is your Collaborative Decision Making strategy?
<--- Score

126. Do you have enough freaky customers in your portfolio pushing you to the limit day in and day out?
<--- Score

127. If you had to leave your organization for a year and the only communication you could have with employees/colleagues was a single paragraph, what would you write?
<--- Score

128. Are the assumptions believable and achievable?
<--- Score

129. Is maximizing Collaborative Decision Making protection the same as minimizing Collaborative Decision Making loss?

<--- Score

130. If you do not follow, then how to lead?
<--- Score

131. How likely is it that a customer would recommend your company to a friend or colleague?
<--- Score

132. Is there any existing Collaborative Decision Making governance structure?
<--- Score

133. How do you govern and fulfill your societal responsibilities?
<--- Score

134. In retrospect, of the projects that you pulled the plug on, what percent do you wish had been allowed to keep going, and what percent do you wish had ended earlier?
<--- Score

135. What goals did you miss?
<--- Score

136. What have been your experiences in defining long range Collaborative Decision Making goals?
<--- Score

137. Operational - will it work?
<--- Score

138. What is the big Collaborative Decision Making idea?
<--- Score

139. How do you stay inspired?
<--- Score

140. What is a feasible sequencing of reform initiatives over time?
<--- Score

141. Why will customers want to buy your organizations products/services?
<--- Score

142. What are the short and long-term Collaborative Decision Making goals?
<--- Score

143. What are the key enablers to make this Collaborative Decision Making move?
<--- Score

144. Did your employees make progress today?
<--- Score

145. Do you have the right capabilities and capacities?
<--- Score

146. What business benefits will Collaborative Decision Making goals deliver if achieved?
<--- Score

147. What are you challenging?
<--- Score

148. Why is Collaborative Decision Making important for you now?
<--- Score

149. How important is Collaborative Decision Making to the user organizations mission?
<--- Score

150. How will you motivate the stakeholders with the least vested interest?
<--- Score

151. If there were zero limitations, what would you do differently?
<--- Score

152. How do you keep records, of what?
<--- Score

153. What are the rules and assumptions your industry operates under? What if the opposite were true?
<--- Score

154. What trouble can you get into?
<--- Score

155. Instead of going to current contacts for new ideas, what if you reconnected with dormant contacts--the people you used to know? If you were going reactivate a dormant tie, who would it be?
<--- Score

156. Who is on the team?
<--- Score

157. What should you stop doing?
<--- Score

158. How do you set Collaborative Decision Making

stretch targets and how do you get people to not only participate in setting these stretch targets but also that they strive to achieve these?
<--- Score

159. If you weren't already in this business, would you enter it today? And if not, what are you going to do about it?
<--- Score

160. Are there any activities that you can take off your to do list?
<--- Score

161. Are assumptions made in Collaborative Decision Making stated explicitly?
<--- Score

162. Who is responsible for Collaborative Decision Making?
<--- Score

163. How can you become more high-tech but still be high touch?
<--- Score

164. Marketing budgets are tighter, consumers are more skeptical, and social media has changed forever the way we talk about Collaborative Decision Making, how do you gain traction?
<--- Score

165. In a project to restructure Collaborative Decision Making outcomes, which stakeholders would you involve?
<--- Score

166. Is your basic point _____ or _____?
<--- Score

167. Are new benefits received and understood?
<--- Score

168. How much does Collaborative Decision Making help?
<--- Score

169. Who do you want your customers to become?
<--- Score

170. If your customer were your grandmother, would you tell her to buy what you're selling?
<--- Score

171. What happens when a new employee joins the organization?
<--- Score

172. What information is critical to your organization that your executives are ignoring?
<--- Score

173. What are the success criteria that will indicate that Collaborative Decision Making objectives have been met and the benefits delivered?
<--- Score

174. What role does communication play in the success or failure of a Collaborative Decision Making project?
<--- Score

175. How do you accomplish your long range Collaborative Decision Making goals?
<--- Score

176. What are the long-term Collaborative Decision Making goals?
<--- Score

177. What are the challenges?
<--- Score

178. What are the top 3 things at the forefront of your Collaborative Decision Making agendas for the next 3 years?
<--- Score

179. What are the essentials of internal Collaborative Decision Making management?
<--- Score

180. What would have to be true for the option on the table to be the best possible choice?
<--- Score

181. What are the gaps in your knowledge and experience?
<--- Score

182. If you got fired and a new hire took your place, what would she do different?
<--- Score

183. How will you know that the Collaborative Decision Making project has been successful?
<--- Score

184. Is Collaborative Decision Making dependent on the successful delivery of a current project?
<--- Score

185. How do you listen to customers to obtain actionable information?
<--- Score

186. Can you maintain your growth without detracting from the factors that have contributed to your success?
<--- Score

187. How do you provide a safe environment -physically and emotionally?
<--- Score

188. What is the overall business strategy?
<--- Score

189. Can you break it down?
<--- Score

190. Will there be any necessary staff changes (redundancies or new hires)?
<--- Score

191. What stupid rule would you most like to kill?
<--- Score

192. Why should you adopt a Collaborative Decision Making framework?
<--- Score

193. Can the schedule be done in the given time?
<--- Score

194. How do you foster innovation?
<--- Score

195. Are you paying enough attention to the partners your company depends on to succeed?
<--- Score

196. How do you transition from the baseline to the target?
<--- Score

197. What are the usability implications of Collaborative Decision Making actions?
<--- Score

198. Do you have an implicit bias for capital investments over people investments?
<--- Score

199. How do senior leaders deploy your organizations vision and values through your leadership system, to the workforce, to key suppliers and partners, and to customers and other stakeholders, as appropriate?
<--- Score

200. What could happen if you do not do it?
<--- Score

201. Ask yourself: how would you do this work if you only had one staff member to do it?
<--- Score

202. Do you see more potential in people than they do in themselves?
<--- Score

203. Think of your Collaborative Decision Making project, what are the main functions?
<--- Score

204. Political -is anyone trying to undermine this project?
<--- Score

205. Does the board have assurance that the information is accurate and complete?
<--- Score

206. Is it economical; do you have the time and money?
<--- Score

207. What is effective Collaborative Decision Making?
<--- Score

208. What are your most important goals for the strategic Collaborative Decision Making objectives?
<--- Score

209. What new services of functionality will be implemented next with Collaborative Decision Making ?
<--- Score

210. If no one would ever find out about your accomplishments, how would you lead differently?
<--- Score

211. What is your question? Why?
<--- Score

212. Are you using a design thinking approach and integrating Innovation, Collaborative Decision Making Experience, and Brand Value?
<--- Score

213. How do you determine the key elements that affect Collaborative Decision Making workforce satisfaction, how are these elements determined for different workforce groups and segments?
<--- Score

214. What happens if you do not have enough funding?
<--- Score

Add up total points for this section:
_____ = Total points for this section

Divided by: _____ (number of statements answered) = _____
Average score for this section

Transfer your score to the Collaborative Decision Making Index at the beginning of the Self-Assessment.

Collaborative Decision Making and Managing Projects, Criteria for Project Managers:

1.0 Initiating Process Group: Collaborative Decision Making

1. Who is funding the Collaborative Decision Making project?

2. What were things that you did well, and could improve, and how?

3. Does the Collaborative Decision Making project team have enough people to execute the Collaborative Decision Making project plan?

4. Have requirements been tested, approved, and fulfill the Collaborative Decision Making project scope?

5. What were things that you need to improve?

6. Are you certain deliverables are properly completed and meet quality standards?

7. Establishment of pm office?

8. Which six sigma dmaic phase focuses on why and how defects and errors occur?

9. Are stakeholders properly informed about the status of the Collaborative Decision Making project?

10. What will be the pressing issues of tomorrow?

11. Will the Collaborative Decision Making project meet the client requirements, and will it achieve the business success criteria that justified doing the

Collaborative Decision Making project in the first place?

12. Are identified risks being monitored properly, are new risks arising during the Collaborative Decision Making project or are foreseen risks occurring?

13. What is the NEXT thing to do?

14. How do you help others satisfy needs?

15. What are the overarching issues of your organization?

16. At which cmmi level are software processes documented, standardized, and integrated into a standard to-be practiced process for your organization?

17. Who supports, improves, and oversees standardized processes related to the Collaborative Decision Making projects program?

18. Specific - is the objective clear in terms of what, how, when, and where the situation will be changed?

19. How will it affect me?

20. During which stage of Risk planning are risks prioritized based on probability and impact?

1.1 Project Charter: Collaborative Decision Making

21. What ideas do you have for initial tests of change (PDSA cycles)?

22. What is in it for you?

23. If finished, on what date did it finish?

24. Name and describe the elements that deal with providing the detail?

25. Customer benefits: what customer requirements does this Collaborative Decision Making project address?

26. Who is the Collaborative Decision Making project Manager?

27. Why do you need to manage scope?

28. Why executive support?

29. What changes can you make to improve?

30. Assumptions: what factors, for planning purposes, are you considering to be true?

31. Collaborative Decision Making project background: what is the primary motivation for this Collaborative Decision Making project?

32. What are some examples of a business case?

33. Who is the sponsor?

34. What is the business need?

35. What are you trying to accomplish?

36. Why have you chosen the aim you have set forth?

37. What is the justification?

38. When is a charter needed?

39. What barriers do you predict to your success?

1.2 Stakeholder Register: Collaborative Decision Making

40. Who is managing stakeholder engagement?

41. What is the power of the stakeholder?

42. How much influence do they have on the Collaborative Decision Making project?

43. What opportunities exist to provide communications?

44. How will reports be created?

45. How should employers make voices heard?

46. Who wants to talk about Security?

47. What are the major Collaborative Decision Making project milestones requiring communications or providing communications opportunities?

48. What & Why?

49. Who are the stakeholders?

50. Is your organization ready for change?

51. How big is the gap?

1.3 Stakeholder Analysis Matrix: Collaborative Decision Making

52. Seasonality, weather effects?

53. Marketing - reach, distribution, awareness?

54. Where are mitigation costs factored in?

55. What makes a person a stakeholder?

56. Timescales, deadlines and pressures?

57. Who can contribute financial or technical resources towards the work?

58. Who will be responsible for managing the outcome?

59. Arena: in what fields are the actors active, where are they present?

60. Insurmountable weaknesses?

61. Are the interests in line with the program objectives?

62. Has there been a similar initiative in the region?

63. It developments?

64. What are the opportunities for communication?

65. Would it be fair to say that cost is a controlling criteria?

66. Who has been involved in the area (thematic or geographic) in the past?

67. Who holds positions of responsibility in interested organizations?

68. Do recommendations include actions to address any differential distribution of impacts?

69. What do you need to appraise?

70. Does the stakeholder want to be involved or merely need to be informed about the Collaborative Decision Making project and its process?

71. If the baseline is now, and if its improved it will be better than now?

2.0 Planning Process Group: Collaborative Decision Making

72. In which Collaborative Decision Making project management process group is the detailed Collaborative Decision Making project budget created?

73. What do they need to know about the Collaborative Decision Making project?

74. Is the Collaborative Decision Making project supported by national and/or local organizations?

75. Professionals want to know what is expected from them; what are the deliverables?

76. Will you be replaced?

77. How are the principles of aid effectiveness (ownership, alignment, management for development results and mutual responsibility) being applied in the Collaborative Decision Making project?

78. Explanation: is what the Collaborative Decision Making project intents to solve a hard question?

79. What input will you be required to provide the Collaborative Decision Making project team?

80. What is involved in Collaborative Decision Making project scope management, and why is good Collaborative Decision Making project

scope management so important on information technology Collaborative Decision Making projects?

81. Have more efficient (sensitive) and appropriate measures been adopted to respond to the political and socio-cultural problems identified?

82. Are there efficient coordination mechanisms to avoid overloading the counterparts, participating stakeholders?

83. Will the products created live up to the necessary quality?

84. What is the difference between the early schedule and late schedule?

85. In what way has the Collaborative Decision Making project come up with innovative measures for problem-solving?

86. Contingency planning. if a risk event occurs, what will you do?

87. First of all, should any action be taken?

88. How many days can task X be late in starting without affecting the Collaborative Decision Making project completion date?

89. To what extent and in what ways are the Collaborative Decision Making project contributing to progress towards organizational reform?

90. Product breakdown structure (pbs): what is the Collaborative Decision Making project result or

product, and how should it look like, what are its parts?

91. What is a Software Development Life Cycle (SDLC)?

2.1 Project Management Plan: Collaborative Decision Making

92. Are alternatives safe, functional, constructible, economical, reasonable and sustainable?

93. When is a Collaborative Decision Making project management plan created?

94. What went right?

95. Is the budget realistic?

96. Is the engineering content at a feasibility level-of-detail, and is it sufficiently complete, to provide an adequate basis for the baseline cost estimate?

97. Is mitigation authorized or recommended?

98. Are there non-structural buyout or relocation recommendations?

99. How well are you able to manage your risk?

100. What are the assigned resources?

101. How do you manage time?

102. Development trends and opportunities. What if the positive direction and vision of your organization causes expected trends to change?

103. Where does all this information come from?

104. How do you organize the costs in the Collaborative Decision Making project management plan?

105. If the Collaborative Decision Making project is complex or scope is specialized, do you have appropriate and/or qualified staff available to perform the tasks?

106. Is there an incremental analysis/cost effectiveness analysis of proposed mitigation features based on an approved method and using an accepted model?

107. What went wrong?

108. What are the assumptions?

109. What would you do differently what did not work?

110. Did the planning effort collaborate to develop solutions that integrate expertise, policies, programs, and Collaborative Decision Making projects across entities?

2.2 Scope Management Plan: Collaborative Decision Making

111. Where do scope processes fit in?

112. Do all stakeholders know how to access this repository and where to find the Collaborative Decision Making project documentation?

113. Will your organizations estimating methodology be used and followed?

114. For which criterion is it tolerable not to meet the original parameters?

115. Does the Collaborative Decision Making project have a Quality Culture?

116. Are action items captured and managed?

117. Have the procedures for identifying budget variances been followed?

118. Given the scope of the Collaborative Decision Making project, which criterion should be optimized?

119. Is a pmo (Collaborative Decision Making project management office) in place and provide oversight to the Collaborative Decision Making project?

120. Has process improvement efforts been completed before requirements efforts begin?

121. Are risk triggers captured?

122. Has a quality assurance plan been developed for the Collaborative Decision Making project?

123. Personnel with expertise?

124. Are the budget estimates reasonable?

125. Can each item be appropriately scheduled?

126. How many changes are you making?

127. Do you document disagreements and work towards resolutions?

128. Are you spending the right amount of money for specific tasks?

129. When will scope verification be performed?

130. Were Collaborative Decision Making project team members involved in the development of activity & task decomposition?

2.3 Requirements Management Plan: Collaborative Decision Making

131. Will you perform a Requirements Risk assessment and develop a plan to deal with risks?

132. Will the Collaborative Decision Making project requirements become approved in writing?

133. Do you really need to write this document at all?

134. Do you understand the role that each stakeholder will play in the requirements process?

135. Did you distinguish the scope of work the contractor(s) will be required to do?

136. Did you get proper approvals?

137. How detailed should the Collaborative Decision Making project get?

138. Business analysis scope?

139. How will requirements be managed?

140. Subject to change control?

141. Will you use an assessment of the Collaborative Decision Making project environment as a tool to discover risk to the requirements process?

142. Is the user satisfied?

143. In case of software development; Should you have a test for each code module?

144. Will you document changes to requirements?

145. Does the Collaborative Decision Making project have a Change Control process?

146. Will you have access to stakeholders when you need them?

147. What is the earliest finish date for this Collaborative Decision Making project if it is scheduled to start on ...?

148. Do you know which stakeholders will participate in the requirements effort?

149. Are actual resources expenditures versus planned expenditures acceptable?

150. How will the requirements become prioritized?

2.4 Requirements Documentation: Collaborative Decision Making

151. How do you get the user to tell you what they want?

152. Are all functions required by the customer included?

153. Do technical resources exist?

154. What if the system wasn t implemented?

155. Validity. does the system provide the functions which best support the customers needs?

156. How much does requirements engineering cost?

157. How can you document system requirements?

158. Who provides requirements?

159. How does what is being described meet the business need?

160. How linear / iterative is your Requirements Gathering process (or will it be)?

161. What is effective documentation?

162. What will be the integration problems?

163. Completeness. are all functions required by the

customer included?

164. Verifiability. can the requirements be checked?

165. What are the potential disadvantages/advantages?

166. Is the origin of the requirement clearly stated?

167. How much testing do you need to do to prove that your system is safe?

168. Can the requirement be changed without a large impact on other requirements?

169. How will the proposed Collaborative Decision Making project help?

170. Is the requirement properly understood?

2.5 Requirements Traceability Matrix: Collaborative Decision Making

171. How do you manage scope?

172. Do you have a clear understanding of all subcontracts in place?

173. Will you use a Requirements Traceability Matrix?

174. What are the chronologies, contingencies, consequences, criteria?

175. Why do you manage scope?

176. Describe the process for approving requirements so they can be added to the traceability matrix and Collaborative Decision Making project work can be performed. Will the Collaborative Decision Making project requirements become approved in writing?

177. How will it affect the stakeholders personally in career?

178. What is the WBS?

179. What percentage of Collaborative Decision Making projects are producing traceability matrices between requirements and other work products?

180. Is there a requirements traceability process in place?

181. Why use a WBS?

182. How small is small enough?

2.6 Project Scope Statement: Collaborative Decision Making

183. Is the plan for your organization of the Collaborative Decision Making project resources adequate?

184. Is there a process (test plans, inspections, reviews) defined for verifying outputs for each task?

185. If there are vendors, have they signed off on the Collaborative Decision Making project Plan?

186. Are there issues that could affect the existing requirements for the result, service, or product if the scope changes?

187. What should you drop in order to add something new?

188. Is this process communicated to the customer and team members?

189. Elements that deal with providing the detail?

190. Has everyone approved the Collaborative Decision Making projects scope statement?

191. Is the scope of your Collaborative Decision Making project well defined?

192. Is there a Quality Assurance Plan documented and filed?

193. Are the meetings set up to have assigned note takers that will add action/issues to the issue list?

194. How often will scope changes be reviewed?

195. Are there backup strategies for key members of the Collaborative Decision Making project?

196. Is there a baseline plan against which to measure progress?

197. Has a method and process for requirement tracking been developed?

198. What is a process you might recommend to verify the accuracy of the research deliverable?

199. What is the most common tool for helping define the detail?

200. If there is an independent oversight contractor, have they signed off on the Collaborative Decision Making project Plan?

2.7 Assumption and Constraint Log: Collaborative Decision Making

201. What do you audit?

202. Can the requirements be traced to the appropriate components of the solution, as well as test scripts?

203. Has a Collaborative Decision Making project Communications Plan been developed?

204. How are new requirements or changes to requirements identified?

205. Have adequate resources been provided by management to ensure Collaborative Decision Making project success?

206. Was the document/deliverable developed per the appropriate or required standards (for example, Institute of Electrical and Electronics Engineers standards)?

207. Has the approach and development strategy of the Collaborative Decision Making project been defined, documented and accepted by the appropriate stakeholders?

208. What would you gain if you spent time working to improve this process?

209. Is the process working, and people are not

executing in compliance of the process?

210. Have all involved stakeholders and work groups committed to the Collaborative Decision Making project?

211. Have all necessary approvals been obtained?

212. What worked well?

213. After observing execution of process, is it in compliance with the documented Plan?

214. Have the scope, objectives, costs, benefits and impacts been communicated to all involved and/or impacted stakeholders and work groups?

215. What strengths do you have?

216. Is the definition of the Collaborative Decision Making project scope clear; what needs to be accomplished?

217. Are there processes defining how software will be developed including development methods, overall timeline for development, software product standards, and traceability?

218. Does the plan conform to standards?

219. Is there documentation of system capability requirements, data requirements, environment requirements, security requirements, and computer and hardware requirements?

2.8 Work Breakdown Structure: Collaborative Decision Making

220. When does it have to be done?

221. Why is it useful?

222. How much detail?

223. How many levels?

224. How big is a work-package?

225. When would you develop a Work Breakdown Structure?

226. What has to be done?

227. Is it a change in scope?

228. Is the work breakdown structure (wbs) defined and is the scope of the Collaborative Decision Making project clear with assigned deliverable owners?

229. Do you need another level?

230. How will you and your Collaborative Decision Making project team define the Collaborative Decision Making projects scope and work breakdown structure?

231. Can you make it?

232. When do you stop?

233. Where does it take place?

234. How far down?

235. Who has to do it?

236. Is it still viable?

237. What is the probability that the Collaborative Decision Making project duration will exceed xx weeks?

2.9 WBS Dictionary: Collaborative Decision Making

238. Are work packages reasonably short in time duration or do they have adequate objective indicators/milestones to minimize subjectivity of the in process work evaluation?

239. Are internal budgets for authorized, and not priced changes based on the contractors resource plan for accomplishing the work?

240. Does the contractors system provide unit or lot costs when applicable?

241. Are current budgets resulting from changes to the authorized work and/or internal replanning, reconcilable to original budgets for specified reporting items?

242. Major functional areas of contract effort?

243. Is subcontracted work defined and identified to the appropriate subcontractor within the proper WBS element?

244. Does the contractor have procedures which permit identification of recurring or non-recurring costs as necessary?

245. Is all budget available as management reserve identified and excluded from the performance measurement baseline?

246. Do the lines of authority for incurring indirect costs correspond to the lines of responsibility for management control of the same components of costs?

247. Are your organizations and items of cost assigned to each pool identified?

248. Are overhead cost budgets (or Collaborative Decision Making projections) established on a facility-wide basis at least annually for the life of the contract?

249. The wbs is developed as part of a joint planning session. and how do you know that youhave done this right?

250. Is all contract work included in the CWBS?

251. Are data being used by managers in an effective manner to ascertain Collaborative Decision Making project or functional status, to identify reasons or significant variance, and to initiate appropriate corrective action?

252. Does the scheduling system provide for the identification of work progress against technical and other milestones, and also provide for forecasts of completion dates of scheduled work?

253. Are overhead budgets and costs being handled according to the disclosure statement when applicable, or otherwise properly classified (for example, engineering overhead, IR&D)?

254. Time-phased control account budgets?

255. Budgeted cost for work performed?

256. What is the end result of a work package?

2.10 Schedule Management Plan: Collaborative Decision Making

257. Staffing Requirements?

258. Are right task and resource calendars used in the IMS?

259. Can additional resources be added to subsequent tasks to reduce the durations of the already stated tasks?

260. Is it standard practice to formally commit stakeholders to the Collaborative Decision Making project via agreements?

261. Has the Collaborative Decision Making project manager been identified?

262. Are Collaborative Decision Making project team members involved in detailed estimating and scheduling?

263. Has your organization readiness assessment been conducted?

264. Have the key elements of a coherent Collaborative Decision Making project management strategy been established?

265. Are all payments made according to the contract(s)?

266. Has a structured approach been used to break work effort into manageable components (WBS)?

267. Are trade-offs between accepting the risk and mitigating the risk identified?

268. Does the Collaborative Decision Making project have a Quality Culture?

269. Are corrective actions and variances reported?

270. Have all unresolved risks been documented?

271. Is there an on-going process in place to monitor Collaborative Decision Making project risks?

272. Is there an approved case?

273. Has a quality assurance plan been developed for the Collaborative Decision Making project?

274. Why time management?

275. Is there a requirements change management processes in place?

276. Are the key elements of a Collaborative Decision Making project Charter present?

2.11 Activity List: Collaborative Decision Making

277. How can the Collaborative Decision Making project be displayed graphically to better visualize the activities?

278. Can you determine the activity that must finish, before this activity can start?

279. How difficult will it be to do specific activities on this Collaborative Decision Making project?

280. When will the work be performed?

281. Where will it be performed?

282. When do the individual activities need to start and finish?

283. Are the required resources available or need to be acquired?

284. What went well?

285. What did not go as well?

286. What will be performed?

287. What is the probability the Collaborative Decision Making project can be completed in xx weeks?

288. What is your organizations history in doing

similar activities?

289. How will it be performed?

290. Who will perform the work?

291. What is the LF and LS for each activity?

292. How much slack is available in the Collaborative Decision Making project?

293. Should you include sub-activities?

294. What is the total time required to complete the Collaborative Decision Making project if no delays occur?

2.12 Activity Attributes: Collaborative Decision Making

295. Activity: what is Missing?

296. How else could the items be grouped?

297. Activity: what is In the Bag?

298. Where else does it apply?

299. Which method produces the more accurate cost assignment?

300. Is there anything planned that does not need to be here?

301. How much activity detail is required?

302. Time for overtime?

303. What conclusions/generalizations can you draw from this?

304. What is the general pattern here?

305. Why?

306. Were there other ways you could have organized the data to achieve similar results?

307. Have you identified the Activity Leveling Priority code value on each activity?

308. Activity: fair or not fair?

309. How difficult will it be to do specific activities on this Collaborative Decision Making project?

310. Does your organization of the data change its meaning?

311. Can more resources be added?

312. Has management defined a definite timeframe for the turnaround or Collaborative Decision Making project window?

313. How many resources do you need to complete the work scope within a limit of X number of days?

2.13 Milestone List: Collaborative Decision Making

314. Political effects?

315. How late can the activity finish?

316. Sustaining internal capabilities?

317. Continuity, supply chain robustness?

318. Gaps in capabilities?

319. How difficult will it be to do specific activities on this Collaborative Decision Making project?

320. How late can each activity be finished and started?

321. Competitive advantages?

322. How soon can the activity finish?

323. What background experience, skills, and strengths does the team bring to your organization?

324. Global influences?

325. It is to be a narrative text providing the crucial aspects of your Collaborative Decision Making project proposal answering what, who, how, when and where?

326. Do you foresee any technical risks or developmental challenges?

327. What are your competitors vulnerabilities?

328. What is the market for your technology, product or service?

329. Level of the Innovation?

330. What would happen if a delivery of material was one week late?

331. When will the Collaborative Decision Making project be complete?

332. What date will the task finish?

2.14 Network Diagram: Collaborative Decision Making

333. Where do schedules come from?

334. What must be completed before an activity can be started?

335. Are you on time?

336. What are the tools?

337. What job or jobs follow it?

338. What job or jobs could run concurrently?

339. What is the probability of completing the Collaborative Decision Making project in less that xx days?

340. Where do you schedule uncertainty time?

341. What activities must occur simultaneously with this activity?

342. Will crashing x weeks return more in benefits than it costs?

343. How difficult will it be to do specific activities on this Collaborative Decision Making project?

344. Are the required resources available?

345. Which type of network diagram allows you to depict four types of dependencies?

346. If the Collaborative Decision Making project network diagram cannot change and you have extra personnel resources, what is the BEST thing to do?

347. What is the completion time?

348. What is the lowest cost to complete this Collaborative Decision Making project in xx weeks?

349. If x is long, what would be the completion time if you break x into two parallel parts of y weeks and z weeks?

350. Planning: who, how long, what to do?

351. What job or jobs precede it?

2.15 Activity Resource Requirements: Collaborative Decision Making

352. Do you use tools like decomposition and rolling-wave planning to produce the activity list and other outputs?

353. How many signatures do you require on a check and does this match what is in your policy and procedures?

354. Are there unresolved issues that need to be addressed?

355. Other support in specific areas?

356. Organizational Applicability?

357. Which logical relationship does the PDM use most often?

358. Anything else?

359. Why do you do that?

360. When does monitoring begin?

361. What are constraints that you might find during the Human Resource Planning process?

362. How do you handle petty cash?

363. What is the Work Plan Standard?

2.16 Resource Breakdown Structure: Collaborative Decision Making

364. What can you do to improve productivity?

365. Who will use the system?

366. What defines a successful Collaborative Decision Making project?

367. How difficult will it be to do specific activities on this Collaborative Decision Making project?

368. Who is allowed to perform which functions?

369. Who needs what information?

370. Why is this important?

371. What defines a successful Collaborative Decision Making project?

372. The list could probably go on, but, the thing that you would most like to know is, How long & How much?

373. Who delivers the information?

374. Why do you do it?

375. What is the purpose of assigning and documenting responsibility?

376. Who will be used as a Collaborative Decision Making project team member?

377. What is the number one predictor of a groups productivity?

378. Is predictive resource analysis being done?

379. What is Collaborative Decision Making project communication management?

2.17 Activity Duration Estimates: Collaborative Decision Making

380. What is the duration of the critical path for this Collaborative Decision Making project?

381. When a risk event occurs, is the risk response evaluated and the appropriate response implemented?

382. What should be done NEXT?

383. Are the causes of all variances identified?

384. Will additional funds be needed for hardware or software?

385. Is a standard form used to obtain bids and proposals from prospective sellers?

386. Research risk management software. Are many products available?

387. Is a contract change control system defined to manage changes to contract terms and conditions?

388. Are costs that may be needed to account for Collaborative Decision Making project risks determined?

389. How difficult will it be to complete specific activities on this Collaborative Decision Making project?

390. When would a milestone chart be used instead of a bar char?

391. Does a process exist to determine the potential loss or gain if risk events occur?

392. What tasks can take place concurrently?

393. What time management activity should you do NEXT?

394. Given your research into similar classes and the work you think is required for this Collaborative Decision Making project, what assumptions, variables, or costs would you change from the information provided above?

395. How does the job market and current state of the economy affect human resource management?

396. Are time, scope, cost, and quality monitored throughout the Collaborative Decision Making project?

397. Is the Collaborative Decision Making project performing better or worse than planned?

398. How could you define throughput and how would your organization benefit from maximizing it?

2.18 Duration Estimating Worksheet: Collaborative Decision Making

399. Small or large Collaborative Decision Making project?

400. What is your role?

401. For other activities, how much delay can be tolerated?

402. Do any colleagues have experience with your organization and/or RFPs?

403. Is this operation cost effective?

404. Science = process: remember the scientific method?

405. How can the Collaborative Decision Making project be displayed graphically to better visualize the activities?

406. What is cost and Collaborative Decision Making project cost management?

407. What info is needed?

408. Define the work as completely as possible. What work will be included in the Collaborative Decision Making project?

409. What utility impacts are there?

410. What work will be included in the Collaborative Decision Making project?

411. Is the Collaborative Decision Making project responsive to community need?

412. How should ongoing costs be monitored to try to keep the Collaborative Decision Making project within budget?

413. What questions do you have?

414. Done before proceeding with this activity or what can be done concurrently?

415. Is a construction detail attached (to aid in explanation)?

2.19 Project Schedule: Collaborative Decision Making

416. Month Collaborative Decision Making project take?

417. Is the Collaborative Decision Making project schedule available for all Collaborative Decision Making project team members to review?

418. What documents, if any, will the subcontractor provide (eg Collaborative Decision Making project schedule, quality plan etc)?

419. Does the condition or event threaten the Collaborative Decision Making projects objectives in any ways?

420. Why is software Collaborative Decision Making project disaster so common?

421. Have all Collaborative Decision Making project delays been adequately accounted for, communicated to all stakeholders and adjustments made in overall Collaborative Decision Making project schedule?

422. Understand the constraints used in preparing the schedule. Are activities connected because logic dictates the order in which others occur?

423. Are quality inspections and review activities listed in the Collaborative Decision Making project schedule(s)?

424. What is the most mis-scheduled part of process?

425. Meet requirements?

426. Activity charts and bar charts are graphical representations of a Collaborative Decision Making project schedule ...how do they differ?

427. Is infrastructure setup part of your Collaborative Decision Making project?

428. How can you address that situation?

429. How can slack be negative?

430. Master Collaborative Decision Making project schedule?

431. How do you know that youhave done this right?

432. Collaborative Decision Making project work estimates Who is managing the work estimate quality of work tasks in the Collaborative Decision Making project schedule?

2.20 Cost Management Plan: Collaborative Decision Making

433. Are software metrics formally captured, analyzed and used as a basis for other Collaborative Decision Making project estimates?

434. Scope of work – What is the scope of work for each of the planned contracts?

435. Will the forecasts be based on trend analysis and earned value statistics?

436. How difficult will it be to do specific tasks on the Collaborative Decision Making project?

437. What are the Collaborative Decision Making project objectives?

438. Have activity relationships and interdependencies within tasks been adequately identified?

439. Is your organization certified as a broker of the products/supplies?

440. Are the Collaborative Decision Making project team members located locally to the users/stakeholders?

441. What is cost and Collaborative Decision Making project cost management?

442. Are target dates established for each milestone deliverable?

443. Contingency rundown curve be used on the Collaborative Decision Making project?

444. Escalation criteria met?

445. What is Collaborative Decision Making project management?

446. Are quality inspections and review activities listed in the Collaborative Decision Making project schedule(s)?

447. Have adequate resources been provided by management to ensure Collaborative Decision Making project success?

448. Has a capability assessment been conducted?

449. Does the resource management plan include a personnel development plan?

450. Are the key elements of a Collaborative Decision Making project Charter present?

451. Has the Collaborative Decision Making project manager been identified?

2.21 Activity Cost Estimates: Collaborative Decision Making

452. What is a Collaborative Decision Making project Management Plan?

453. Review – what are some common errors in activities to avoid?

454. Can you delete activities or make them inactive?

455. What is the activity inventory?

456. What areas does the group agree are the biggest success on the Collaborative Decision Making project?

457. How do you manage cost?

458. Estimated cost?

459. How do you allocate indirect costs to activities?

460. Are cost subtotals needed?

461. Was the consultant knowledgeable about the program?

462. What were things that you did very well and want to do the same again on the next Collaborative Decision Making project?

463. How do you fund change orders?

464. Eac -estimate at completion, what is the total job expected to cost?

465. The impact and what actions were taken?

466. Where can you get activity reports?

467. Are data needed on characteristics of care?

468. Measurable - are the targets measurable?

469. Were you satisfied with the work?

470. What are you looking for?

2.22 Cost Estimating Worksheet: Collaborative Decision Making

471. Does the Collaborative Decision Making project provide innovative ways for stakeholders to overcome obstacles or deliver better outcomes?

472. Can a trend be established from historical performance data on the selected measure and are the criteria for using trend analysis or forecasting methods met?

473. Identify the timeframe necessary to monitor progress and collect data to determine how the selected measure has changed?

474. Who is best positioned to know and assist in identifying corresponding factors?

475. Will the Collaborative Decision Making project collaborate with the local community and leverage resources?

476. What is the estimated labor cost today based upon this information?

477. What happens to any remaining funds not used?

478. Ask: are others positioned to know, are others credible, and will others cooperate?

479. What can be included?

480. Is the Collaborative Decision Making project responsive to community need?

481. Value pocket identification & quantification what are value pockets?

482. What will others want?

483. How will the results be shared and to whom?

484. What costs are to be estimated?

485. What is the purpose of estimating?

486. What additional Collaborative Decision Making project(s) could be initiated as a result of this Collaborative Decision Making project?

487. Is it feasible to establish a control group arrangement?

2.23 Cost Baseline: Collaborative Decision Making

488. What can go wrong?

489. If you sold 10x widgets on a day, what would the affect on profits be?

490. What does a good WBS NOT look like?

491. How long are you willing to wait before you find out were late?

492. Are you meeting with your team regularly?

493. At which frequency ?

494. Where do changes come from?

495. Has the appropriate access to relevant data and analysis capability been granted?

496. Will the Collaborative Decision Making project fail if the change request is not executed?

497. What is cost and Collaborative Decision Making project cost management?

498. Has the documentation relating to operation and maintenance of the product(s) or service(s) been delivered to, and accepted by, operations management?

499. What weaknesses do you have?

500. Does it impact schedule, cost, quality?

501. Should a more thorough impact analysis be conducted?

502. How will cost estimates be used?

503. How likely is it to go wrong?

504. Have all approved changes to the schedule baseline been identified and impact on the Collaborative Decision Making project documented?

2.24 Quality Management Plan: Collaborative Decision Making

505. How do your action plans support the strategic objectives?

506. Written by multiple authors and in multiple writing styles?

507. What is the return on investment?

508. How do you check in-coming sample material?

509. What are your organizations current levels and trends for the already stated measures related to employee wellbeing, satisfaction, and development?

510. Is there a Steering Committee in place?

511. Have all involved stakeholders and work groups committed to the Collaborative Decision Making project?

512. How is staff trained in procedures?

513. What is quality and how will you ensure it?

514. Contradictory information between different documents?

515. Are qmps good forever?

516. Is a component/condition present?

517. How does your organization use comparative data and information to improve organizational performance?

518. Is there a Quality Management Plan?

519. Are you meeting your customers expectations consistently?

520. How does your organization manage work to promote cooperation, individual initiative, innovation, flexibility, communications, and knowledge/skill sharing across work units?

521. No superfluous information or marketing narrative?

522. How will you know that a change is actually an improvement?

523. Can you perform this task or activity in a more effective manner?

524. Why quality management?

2.25 Quality Metrics: Collaborative Decision Making

525. How does one achieve stability?

526. Was review conducted per standard protocols?

527. Are there already quality metrics available that detect nonlinear embeddings and trends similar to the users perception?

528. What is the benchmark?

529. Where did complaints, returns and warranty claims come from?

530. When is the security analysis testing complete?

531. What documentation is required?

532. What method of measurement do you use?

533. What makes a visualization memorable?

534. Which report did you use to create the data you are submitting?

535. Have risk areas been identified?

536. What can manufacturing professionals do to ensure quality is seen as an integral part of the entire product lifecycle?

537. How do you know if everyone is trying to improve the right things?

538. Is the reporting frequency appropriate?

539. If the defect rate during testing is substantially higher than that of the previous release (or a similar product), then ask: Did you plan for and actually improve testing effectiveness?

540. What level of statistical confidence do you use?

541. Do the operators focus on determining; is there anything you need to worry about?

542. Where is quality now?

543. Is quality culture a competitive advantage?

544. What are your organizations expectations for its quality Collaborative Decision Making project?

2.26 Process Improvement Plan: Collaborative Decision Making

545. The motive is determined by asking, Why do you want to achieve this goal?

546. Where do you focus?

547. What actions are needed to address the problems and achieve the goals?

548. Does explicit definition of the measures exist?

549. Has a process guide to collect the data been developed?

550. Are you meeting the quality standards?

551. What is the test-cycle concept?

552. Are you making progress on the improvement framework?

553. What personnel are the coaches for your initiative?

554. Are you making progress on your improvement plan?

555. Are you making progress on the goals?

556. How do you manage quality?

557. If a process improvement framework is being used, which elements will help the problems and goals listed?

558. What personnel are the sponsors for that initiative?

559. What lessons have you learned so far?

560. What personnel are the champions for the initiative?

561. Why do you want to achieve the goal?

562. Purpose of goal: the motive is determined by asking, why do you want to achieve this goal?

2.27 Responsibility Assignment Matrix: Collaborative Decision Making

563. What simple tool can you use to help identify and prioritize Collaborative Decision Making project risks that is very low tech and high touch?

564. Are control accounts opened and closed based on the start and completion of work contained therein?

565. All cwbs elements specified for external reporting?

566. Are the actual costs used for variance analysis reconcilable with data from the accounting system?

567. What will the work cost?

568. Too many is: do all the identified roles need to be routinely informed or only in exceptional circumstances?

569. Are material costs reported within the same period as that in which BCWP is earned for that material?

570. Which Collaborative Decision Making project management knowledge area is least mature?

571. What are the deliverables?

572. Are records maintained to show how management reserves are used?

573. Are the overhead pools formally and adequately identified?

574. Are authorized changes being incorporated in a timely manner?

575. How many hours by each staff member/rate?

576. Are indirect costs charged to the appropriate indirect pools and incurring organization?

577. Are others working on the right things?

578. Is the anticipated (firm and potential) business base Collaborative Decision Making projected in a rational, consistent manner?

579. Are estimates of costs at completion generated in a rational, consistent manner?

580. Past experience – the person or the group worked at something similar in the past?

581. What are some important Collaborative Decision Making project communications management tools?

2.28 Roles and Responsibilities: Collaborative Decision Making

582. What specific behaviors did you observe?

583. Key conclusions and recommendations: Are conclusions and recommendations relevant and acceptable?

584. What are your major roles and responsibilities in the area of performance measurement and assessment?

585. Are Collaborative Decision Making project team roles and responsibilities identified and documented?

586. Be specific; avoid generalities. Thank you and great work alone are insufficient. What exactly do you appreciate and why?

587. Once the responsibilities are defined for the Collaborative Decision Making project, have the deliverables, roles and responsibilities been clearly communicated to every participant?

588. Do the values and practices inherent in the culture of your organization foster or hinder the process?

589. Have you ever been a part of this team?

590. What is working well?

591. Required skills, knowledge, experience?

592. Influence: what areas of organizational decision making are you able to influence when you do not have authority to make the final decision?

593. What expectations were met?

594. Who is responsible for implementation activities and where will the functions, roles and responsibilities be defined?

595. Was the expectation clearly communicated?

596. Are your policies supportive of a culture of quality data?

597. Who: who is involved?

598. To decide whether to use a quality measurement, ask how will you know when it is achieved?

599. Who is responsible for each task?

600. How is your work-life balance?

2.29 Human Resource Management Plan: Collaborative Decision Making

601. Do all stakeholders know how to access this repository and where to find the Collaborative Decision Making project documentation?

602. How are superior performers differentiated from average performers?

603. Are vendor contract reports, reviews and visits conducted periodically?

604. Are metrics used to evaluate and manage Vendors?

605. Do people have the competencies to meet the strategic objectives?

606. Does the Collaborative Decision Making project have a formal Collaborative Decision Making project Charter?

607. Has a Collaborative Decision Making project Communications Plan been developed?

608. Quality of people required to meet the forecast needs of the department?

609. How are you going to ensure that you have a well motivated workforce?

610. Have all involved Collaborative Decision Making

project stakeholders and work groups committed to the Collaborative Decision Making project?

611. Is this Collaborative Decision Making project carried out in partnership with other groups/ organizations?

612. Have Collaborative Decision Making project success criteria been defined?

613. Collaborative Decision Making project definition & scope?

614. Are tasks tracked by hours?

615. Are changes in deliverable commitments agreed to by all affected groups & individuals?

616. Have stakeholder accountabilities & responsibilities been clearly defined?

617. Has a resource management plan been created?

618. Is it possible to track all classes of Collaborative Decision Making project work (e.g. scheduled, unscheduled, defect repair, etc.)?

619. Was the scope definition used in task sequencing?

2.30 Communications Management Plan: Collaborative Decision Making

620. Will messages be directly related to the release strategy or phases of the Collaborative Decision Making project?

621. Why is stakeholder engagement important?

622. Are you constantly rushing from meeting to meeting?

623. How were corresponding initiatives successful?

624. Are others needed?

625. Who to share with?

626. Is the stakeholder role recognized by your organization?

627. Where do team members get information?

628. Conflict resolution -which method when?

629. How is this initiative related to other portfolios, programs, or Collaborative Decision Making projects?

630. What communications method?

631. How will the person responsible for executing the communication item be notified?

632. Who to learn from?

633. Do you then often overlook a key stakeholder or stakeholder group?

634. Which team member will work with each stakeholder?

635. Are others part of the communications management plan?

636. How did the term stakeholder originate?

637. What is the political influence?

638. Who is the stakeholder?

2.31 Risk Management Plan: Collaborative Decision Making

639. What can you do to minimize the impact if it does?

640. Are the participants able to keep up with the workload?

641. Are certain activities taking a long time to complete?

642. Are flexibility and reuse paramount?

643. Technology risk: is the Collaborative Decision Making project technically feasible?

644. Have top software and customer managers formally committed to support the Collaborative Decision Making project?

645. Was an original risk assessment/risk management plan completed?

646. Who should be notified of the occurrence of each of the indicators?

647. Havent software Collaborative Decision Making projects been late before?

648. What are the chances the event will occur?

649. Does the Collaborative Decision Making project

team have experience with the technology to be implemented?

650. Are there risks to human health or the environment that need to be controlled or mitigated?

651. What would you do?

652. Are the reports useful and easy to read?

653. Which is an input to the risk management process?

654. Are you working on the right risks?

655. Management -what contingency plans do you have if the risk becomes a reality?

656. What are it-specific requirements?

657. Do you have a mechanism for managing change?

658. Does the Collaborative Decision Making project have the authority and ability to avoid the risk?

2.32 Risk Register: Collaborative Decision Making

659. Risk probability and impact: how will the probabilities and impacts of risk items be assessed?

660. Can the likelihood and impact of failing to achieve corresponding recommendations and action plans be assessed?

661. Risk documentation: what reporting formats and processes will be used for risk management activities?

662. What is the reason for current performance gaps and do the risks and opportunities identified previously account for this?

663. How could corresponding Risk affect the Collaborative Decision Making project in terms of cost and schedule?

664. What should you do when?

665. What may happen or not go according to plan?

666. How are risks identified?

667. Who is accountable?

668. Are there any gaps in the evidence?

669. What should the audit role be in establishing a risk management process?

670. Financial risk -can your organization afford to undertake the Collaborative Decision Making project?

671. What is a Risk?

672. Contingency actions - planned actions to reduce the immediate seriousness of the risk when it does occur. What should you do when?

673. What should you do now?

674. Are corrective measures implemented as planned?

675. Are there any knock-on effects/impact on any of the other areas?

676. Are your objectives at risk?

677. What further options might be available for responding to the risk?

678. What risks might negatively or positively affect achieving the Collaborative Decision Making project objectives?

2.33 Probability and Impact Assessment: Collaborative Decision Making

679. Are tool mentors available?

680. Does the customer understand the software process?

681. Do you have a consistent repeatable process that is actually used?

682. Are there any Collaborative Decision Making projects similar to this one in existence?

683. My Collaborative Decision Making project leader has suddenly left your organization, what do you do?

684. Have you ascribed a level of confidence to every critical technical objective?

685. What new technologies are being explored in the same area?

686. Can the risk be avoided by choosing a different alternative?

687. How completely has the customer been identified?

688. Are there new risks that mitigation strategies might introduce?

689. What is the probability of the risk occurring?

690. Do you have specific methods that you use for each phase of the process?

691. Which role do you have in the Collaborative Decision Making project?

692. Risks should be identified during which phase of Collaborative Decision Making project management life cycle?

693. Are tools for analysis and design available?

694. What should be the gestation period for the Collaborative Decision Making project with specific technology?

695. Can the Collaborative Decision Making project proceed without assuming the risk?

696. How well is the risk understood?

697. Risk categorization -which of your categories has more risk than others?

2.34 Probability and Impact Matrix: Collaborative Decision Making

698. Is there any sign of biased ranking?

699. How are risks and risk management perceived in the Collaborative Decision Making project?

700. Degree of confidence in estimated size estimate?

701. What should you do FIRST?

702. While preparing your risk responses, you identify additional risks. What should you do?

703. How can you understand and diagnose risks and identify sources?

704. Do end-users have realistic expectations?

705. Mitigation -how can you avoid the risk?

706. What will the damage be?

707. Are some people working on multiple Collaborative Decision Making projects?

708. If you can not fix it, how do you do it differently?

709. How would you suggest monitoring for risk transition indicators?

710. How do you analyze the risks in the different

types of Collaborative Decision Making projects?

711. Is the customer willing to establish rapid communication links with the developer?

712. What would you do differently?

713. Could others have been better mitigated?

714. What is the best method for analysing the risks for different types of Collaborative Decision Making projects?

2.35 Risk Data Sheet: Collaborative Decision Making

715. What was measured?

716. What is the chance that it will happen?

717. What can happen?

718. How can hazards be reduced?

719. What will be the consequences if the risk happens?

720. Whom do you serve (customers)?

721. Do effective diagnostic tests exist?

722. Is the data sufficiently specified in terms of the type of failure being analyzed, and its frequency or probability?

723. Has a sensitivity analysis been carried out?

724. What are you trying to achieve (Objectives)?

725. Are new hazards created?

726. How can it happen?

727. What if client refuses?

728. During work activities could hazards exist?

729. What is the environment within which you operate (social trends, economic, community values, broad based participation, national directions etc.)?

730. How reliable is the data source?

731. What are you here for (Mission)?

732. What do people affected think about the need for, and practicality of preventive measures?

733. What are you weak at and therefore need to do better?

2.36 Procurement Management Plan: Collaborative Decision Making

734. Are any non-compliance issues that exist communicated to your organization?

735. What areas are overlooked on this Collaborative Decision Making project?

736. Are the Collaborative Decision Making project plans updated on a frequent basis?

737. What were things that you did very well and want to do the same again on the next Collaborative Decision Making project?

738. Has the budget been baselined?

739. Does the Collaborative Decision Making project have a Statement of Work?

740. How long will it take for the purchase cost to be the same as the lease cost?

741. Are vendor invoices audited for accuracy before payment?

742. Are decisions made in a timely manner?

743. Are changes in scope (deliverable commitments) agreed to by all affected groups & individuals?

744. Is there a procurement management plan in

place?

745. Have lessons learned been conducted after each Collaborative Decision Making project release?

746. Are the quality tools and methods identified in the Quality Plan appropriate to the Collaborative Decision Making project?

747. Does the Collaborative Decision Making project team have the right skills?

748. Are multiple estimation methods being employed?

749. Is Collaborative Decision Making project status reviewed with the steering and executive teams at appropriate intervals?

750. How will you coordinate Procurement with aspects of the Collaborative Decision Making project?

751. Does all Collaborative Decision Making project documentation reside in a common repository for easy access?

752. Is there an on-going process in place to monitor Collaborative Decision Making project risks?

2.37 Source Selection Criteria: Collaborative Decision Making

753. Have all evaluators been trained?

754. In order of importance, which evaluation criteria are the most critical to the determination of your overall rating?

755. Is the offeror pricing what is technically proposed?

756. Can you make a cost/technical tradeoff?

757. Do you consider all weaknesses, significant weaknesses, and deficiencies?

758. Is there collaboration among your evaluators?

759. What instructions should be provided regarding oral presentations?

760. Does the evaluation of any change include an impact analysis; how will the change affect the scope, time, cost, and quality of the goods or services being provided?

761. What information is to be provided and when should it be provided?

762. What are the most common types of rating systems?

763. How should oral presentations be evaluated?

764. How can solicitation Schedules be improved to yield more effective price competition?

765. How should the solicitation aspects regarding past performance be structured?

766. What can not be disclosed?

767. Is a letter of commitment from each proposed team member and key subcontractor included?

768. What are open book debriefings?

769. What are the guidelines regarding award without considerations?

770. What should a Draft Request for Proposal (DRFP) include?

771. How much past performance information should be requested?

772. When should debriefings be held and how should they be scheduled?

2.38 Stakeholder Management Plan: Collaborative Decision Making

773. Are post milestone Collaborative Decision Making project reviews (PMPR) conducted with your organization at least once a year?

774. What are reporting requirements?

775. What is the drawback in using qualitative Collaborative Decision Making project selection techniques?

776. What procedures will be utilised to ensure effective monitoring of Collaborative Decision Making project progress?

777. Have all stakeholders been identified?

778. Are there nonconformance issues?

779. Is stakeholder involvement adequate?

780. Has the business need been clearly defined?

781. Who might be involved in developing a charter?

782. Is there a formal set of procedures supporting Stakeholder Management?

783. Was trending evident between audits?

784. Are enough systems & user personnel assigned

to the Collaborative Decision Making project?

785. Will all relevant stakeholders be included within the review process?

786. Have all team members been part of identifying risks?

787. Does the Collaborative Decision Making project have a Statement of Work?

788. Are there unnecessary steps that are creating bottlenecks and/or causing people to wait?

789. How many Collaborative Decision Making project staff does this specific process affect?

2.39 Change Management Plan: Collaborative Decision Making

790. How much change management is needed?

791. How prevalent is Resistance to Change?

792. Have the business unit contacts been selected and notified?

793. Who will do the training?

794. What risks may occur upfront?

795. Where will the funds come from?

796. Will all field readiness criteria have been practically met prior to training roll-out?

797. What is the worst thing that can happen if you communicate information?

798. What work practices will be affected?

799. What can you do to minimise misinterpretation and negative perceptions?

800. What policies and procedures need to be changed?

801. What communication network would you use – informal or formal?

802. Is there support for this application(s) and are the details available for distribution?

803. Where do you want to be?

804. What are the responsibilities assigned to each role?

805. What goal(s) do you hope to accomplish?

806. What relationships will change?

807. How will you deal with anger about the restricting of communications due to confidentiality considerations?

808. Do you need a new organization structure?

3.0 Executing Process Group: Collaborative Decision Making

809. Are escalated issues resolved promptly?

810. When is the appropriate time to bring the scorecard to Board meetings?

811. Does software appear easy to learn?

812. Are the necessary foundations in place to ensure the sustainability of the results of the programme?

813. What will you do to minimize the impact should a risk event occur?

814. Why is it important to determine activity sequencing on Collaborative Decision Making projects?

815. Why should Collaborative Decision Making project managers strive to make jobs look easy?

816. How can software assist in procuring goods and services?

817. How well did the chosen processes fit the needs of the Collaborative Decision Making project?

818. Do the products created live up to the necessary quality?

819. What Collaborative Decision Making projects and

services are in the portfolio of your organization?

820. What are the main types of contracts if you do decide to outsource?

821. How well defined and documented were the Collaborative Decision Making project management processes you chose to use?

822. Do your results resemble a normal distribution?

823. How do you enter durations, link tasks, and view critical path information?

824. If a risk event occurs, what will you do?

825. What communication items need improvement?

826. What are the critical steps involved with strategy mapping?

827. What are the Collaborative Decision Making project management deliverables of each process group?

3.1 Team Member Status Report: Collaborative Decision Making

828. Does your organization have the means (staff, money, contract, etc.) to produce or to acquire the product, good, or service?

829. How will resource planning be done?

830. Does every department have to have a Collaborative Decision Making project Manager on staff?

831. What specific interest groups do you have in place?

832. Why is it to be done?

833. Do you have an Enterprise Collaborative Decision Making project Management Office (EPMO)?

834. Does the product, good, or service already exist within your organization?

835. Are your organizations Collaborative Decision Making projects more successful over time?

836. How much risk is involved?

837. Is there evidence that staff is taking a more professional approach toward management of your organizations Collaborative Decision Making projects?

838. When a teams productivity and success depend on collaboration and the efficient flow of information, what generally fails them?

839. Are the products of your organizations Collaborative Decision Making projects meeting customers objectives?

840. The problem with Reward & Recognition Programs is that the truly deserving people all too often get left out. How can you make it practical?

841. What is to be done?

842. Will the staff do training or is that done by a third party?

843. How can you make it practical?

844. Are the attitudes of staff regarding Collaborative Decision Making project work improving?

845. How does this product, good, or service meet the needs of the Collaborative Decision Making project and your organization as a whole?

846. How it is to be done?

3.2 Change Request: Collaborative Decision Making

847. How many times must the change be modified or presented to the change control board before it is approved?

848. How is the change documented (format, content, storage)?

849. Will new change requests be acknowledged in a timely manner?

850. What is the purpose of change control?

851. Can you answer what happened, who did it, when did it happen, and what else will be affected?

852. Are you implementing itil processes?

853. Which requirements attributes affect the risk to reliability the most?

854. Who is responsible to authorize changes?

855. How is quality being addressed on the Collaborative Decision Making project?

856. Customer acceptance plan how will the customer verify the change has been implemented successfully?

857. Does the schedule include Collaborative Decision

Making project management time and change request analysis time?

858. How does your organization control changes before and after software is released to a customer?

859. Who needs to approve change requests?

860. Can static requirements change attributes like the size of the change be used to predict reliability in execution?

861. What is the relationship between requirements attributes and reliability?

862. Has your address changed?

863. Who can suggest changes?

864. How well do experienced software developers predict software change?

865. What has an inspector to inspect and to check?

866. Why do you want to have a change control system?

3.3 Change Log: Collaborative Decision Making

867. Is this a mandatory replacement?

868. Who initiated the change request?

869. Does the suggested change request represent a desired enhancement to the products functionality?

870. When was the request approved?

871. When was the request submitted?

872. How does this change affect scope?

873. Is the change request within Collaborative Decision Making project scope?

874. Is the change backward compatible without limitations?

875. How does this change affect the timeline of the schedule?

876. Is the change request open, closed or pending?

877. Is the submitted change a new change or a modification of a previously approved change?

878. How does this relate to the standards developed for specific business processes?

879. Does the suggested change request seem to represent a necessary enhancement to the product?

880. Is the requested change request a result of changes in other Collaborative Decision Making project(s)?

881. Will the Collaborative Decision Making project fail if the change request is not executed?

882. Do the described changes impact on the integrity or security of the system?

3.4 Decision Log: Collaborative Decision Making

883. How do you know when you are achieving it?

884. How does an increasing emphasis on cost containment influence the strategies and tactics used?

885. Which variables make a critical difference?

886. Behaviors; what are guidelines that the team has identified that will assist them with getting the most out of team meetings?

887. At what point in time does loss become unacceptable?

888. Who will be given a copy of this document and where will it be kept?

889. Linked to original objective?

890. Decision-making process; how will the team make decisions?

891. How do you define success?

892. Who is the decisionmaker?

893. With whom was the decision shared or considered?

894. How consolidated and comprehensive a story can you tell by capturing currently available incident data in a central location and through a log of key decisions during an incident?

895. What are the cost implications?

896. How does provision of information, both in terms of content and presentation, influence acceptance of alternative strategies?

897. Meeting purpose; why does this team meet?

898. How effective is maintaining the log at facilitating organizational learning?

899. What alternatives/risks were considered?

900. Is your opponent open to a non-traditional workflow, or will it likely challenge anything you do?

901. What was the rationale for the decision?

902. What is the average size of your matters in an applicable measurement?

3.5 Quality Audit: Collaborative Decision Making

903. Can your organization demonstrate exactly how and why results were achieved?

904. What review processes are in place for your organizations major activities?

905. How does the organization know that its system for maintaining and advancing the capabilities of its staff, particularly in relation to the Mission of the organization, is appropriately effective and constructive?

906. How well do you think your organization engages with the outside community?

907. How does your organization know that its staff entrance standards are appropriately effective and constructive and being implemented consistently?

908. Are multiple statements on the same issue consistent with each other?

909. Does everyone know what they are supposed to be doing, how and why?

910. How does your organization ensure that equipment is appropriately maintained and producing valid results?

911. How does your organization know that its

Governance system is appropriately effective and constructive?

912. How does your organization know that its Mission, Vision and Values Statements are appropriate and effectively guiding your organization?

913. What does the organizarion look for in a Quality audit?

914. Is progress against the intentions measurable?

915. Is the continuing professional education of key personnel account fored in detail?

916. Does the audit organization have experience in performing the required work for entities of your type and size?

917. Does the report read coherently?

918. Is your organizational structure a help or a hindrance to deployment?

919. Does the suppliers quality system have a written procedure for corrective action when a defect occurs?

920. How does your organization know that its system for managing intellectual property issues is appropriately effective, constructive and fair?

921. How does your organization know that its teaching activities (and staff learning) are effectively and constructively enhanced by its activities?

3.6 Team Directory: Collaborative Decision Making

922. When does information need to be distributed?

923. Process decisions: are there any statutory or regulatory issues relevant to the timely execution of work?

924. When will you produce deliverables?

925. Does a Collaborative Decision Making project team directory list all resources assigned to the Collaborative Decision Making project?

926. Where will the product be used and/or delivered or built when appropriate?

927. Process decisions: is work progressing on schedule and per contract requirements?

928. Why is the work necessary?

929. Process decisions: are all start-up, turn over and close out requirements of the contract satisfied?

930. Who will report Collaborative Decision Making project status to all stakeholders?

931. Process decisions: are contractors adequately prosecuting the work?

932. Who will write the meeting minutes and

distribute?

933. How will the team handle changes?

934. How does the team resolve conflicts and ensure tasks are completed?

935. Process decisions: do job conditions warrant additional actions to collect job information and document on-site activity?

936. Decisions: what could be done better to improve the quality of the constructed product?

937. Who are the Team Members?

938. Where should the information be distributed?

939. Decisions: is the most suitable form of contract being used?

3.7 Team Operating Agreement: Collaborative Decision Making

940. Methodologies: how will key team processes be implemented, such as training, research, work deliverable production, review and approval processes, knowledge management, and meeting procedures?

941. Do you send out the agenda and meeting materials in advance?

942. What is teaming?

943. What is your unique contribution to your organization?

944. Are there differences in access to communication and collaboration technology based on team member location?

945. How will group handle unplanned absences?

946. Conflict resolution: how will disputes and other conflicts be mediated or resolved?

947. Do team members need to frequently communicate as a full group to make timely decisions?

948. Do you leverage technology engagement tools group chat, polls, screen sharing, etc.?

949. What individual strengths does each team member bring to the group?

950. What is group supervision?

951. Do you use a parking lot for any items that are important and outside of the agenda?

952. Did you draft the meeting agenda?

953. Do you vary your voice pace, tone and pitch to engage participants and gain involvement?

954. The method to be used in the decision making process; Will it be consensus, majority rule, or the supervisor having the final say?

955. How do you want to be thought of and known within your organization?

956. Do you brief absent members after they view meeting notes or listen to a recording?

957. Did you delegate tasks such as taking meeting minutes, presenting a topic and soliciting input?

958. Confidentiality: how will confidential information be handled?

959. Do you begin with a question to engage everyone?

3.8 Team Performance Assessment: Collaborative Decision Making

960. To what degree do team members understand one anothers roles and skills?

961. To what degree does the teams work approach provide opportunity for members to engage in results-based evaluation?

962. Lack of method variance in self-reported affect and perceptions at work: Reality or artifact?

963. To what degree are staff involved as partners in the improvement process?

964. To what degree are the relative importance and priority of the goals clear to all team members?

965. To what degree can the team measure progress against specific goals?

966. How do you recognize and praise members for contributions?

967. To what degree does the teams work approach provide opportunity for members to engage in open interaction?

968. If you have received criticism from reviewers that your work suffered from method variance, what was the circumstance?

969. To what degree will the team ensure that all members equitably share the work essential to the success of the team?

970. To what degree can team members meet frequently enough to accomplish the teams ends?

971. Do friends perform better than acquaintances?

972. To what degree do all members feel responsible for all agreed-upon measures?

973. If you have criticized someones work for method variance in your role as reviewer, what was the circumstance?

974. To what degree do the goals specify concrete team work products?

975. Do you promptly inform members about major developments that may affect them?

976. To what degree will new and supplemental skills be introduced as the need is recognized?

977. How does Collaborative Decision Making project termination impact Collaborative Decision Making project team members?

978. How do you encourage members to learn from each other?

979. To what degree are the members clear on what they are individually responsible for and what they are jointly responsible for?

3.9 Team Member Performance Assessment: Collaborative Decision Making

980. What steps have you taken to improve performance?

981. Can your organization rate by exception and assume that most employees are performing at an acceptable level?

982. What is a significant fact or event?

983. How do you currently use the time that is available?

984. Who they are?

985. What is the role of the Reviewer?

986. Are any governance changes sufficient to impact achievement?

987. To what degree are sub-teams possible or necessary?

988. To what degree does the team possess adequate membership to achieve its ends?

989. Did training work?

990. To what degree are the goals ambitious?

991. To what degree are the skill areas critical to team performance present?

992. What are best practices in use for the performance measurement system?

993. How do you make use of research?

994. How should adaptive assessments be implemented?

995. What entity leads the process, selects a potential restructuring option and develops the plan?

996. What tools are available to determine whether all contract functional and compliance areas of performance objectives, measures, and incentives have been met?

997. Does statute or regulation require the job responsibility?

998. What are the standards or expectations for success?

999. How are evaluation results utilized?

3.10 Issue Log: Collaborative Decision Making

1000. Is access to the Issue Log controlled?

1001. Why not more evaluators?

1002. Is the issue log kept in a safe place?

1003. How much time does it take to do it?

1004. Do you feel more overwhelmed by stakeholders?

1005. What are the stakeholders interrelationships?

1006. What date was the issue resolved?

1007. What is a change?

1008. How were past initiatives successful?

1009. What is the impact on the risks?

1010. Who needs to know and how much?

1011. Why multiple evaluators?

1012. Are they needed?

1013. What is a Stakeholder?

1014. How do you manage human resources?

1015. How is this initiative related to other portfolios, programs, or Collaborative Decision Making projects?

1016. Do you feel a register helps?

4.0 Monitoring and Controlling Process Group: Collaborative Decision Making

1017. How well did the chosen processes produce the expected results?

1018. What resources (both financial and non-financial) are available/needed?

1019. Feasibility: how much money, time, and effort can you put into this?

1020. Were sponsors and decision makers available when needed outside regularly scheduled meetings?

1021. Did it work?

1022. What is the timeline for the Collaborative Decision Making project?

1023. What are the goals of the program?

1024. Change, where should you look for problems?

1025. What input will you be required to provide the Collaborative Decision Making project team?

1026. What resources are necessary?

1027. Is the program making progress in helping to achieve the set results?

1028. How can you monitor progress?

1029. Overall, how does the program function to serve the clients?

1030. In what way has the program come up with innovative measures for problem-solving?

1031. How is Agile Collaborative Decision Making project Management done?

1032. Did the Collaborative Decision Making project team have enough people to execute the Collaborative Decision Making project plan?

1033. How well did the chosen processes fit the needs of the Collaborative Decision Making project?

4.1 Project Performance Report: Collaborative Decision Making

1034. How is the data used?

1035. What is the PRS?

1036. To what degree are the teams goals and objectives clear, simple, and measurable?

1037. To what degree will the team adopt a concrete, clearly understood, and agreed-upon approach that will result in achievement of the teams goals?

1038. To what degree does the task meet individual needs?

1039. To what degree do team members feel that the purpose of the team is important, if not exciting?

1040. To what degree do the relationships of the informal organization motivate taskrelevant behavior and facilitate task completion?

1041. To what degree are the demands of the task compatible with and converge with the mission and functions of the formal organization?

1042. To what degree will team members, individually and collectively, commit time to help themselves and others learn and develop skills?

1043. How can Collaborative Decision Making project

sustainability be maintained?

1044. To what degree does the teams work approach provide opportunity for members to engage in fact-based problem solving?

1045. To what degree does the informal organization make use of individual resources and meet individual needs?

1046. To what degree do team members articulate the teams work approach?

1047. To what degree are the structures of the formal organization consistent with the behaviors in the informal organization?

4.2 Variance Analysis: Collaborative Decision Making

1048. Are management actions taken to reduce indirect costs when there are significant adverse variances?

1049. Are overhead costs budgets established on a basis consistent with the anticipated direct business base?

1050. What is the budgeted cost for work scheduled?

1051. Contract line items and end items?

1052. Who are responsible for overhead performance control of related costs?

1053. What is the expected future profitability of each customer?

1054. Can the relationship with problem customers be restructured so that there is a win-win situation?

1055. How does your organization allocate the cost of shared expenses and services?

1056. Does the contractors system include procedures for measuring the performance of critical subcontractors?

1057. Are the bases and rates for allocating costs from each indirect pool consistently applied?

1058. Are there quarterly budgets with quarterly performance comparisons?

1059. Are all authorized tasks assigned to identified organizational elements?

1060. Are procedures for variance analysis documented and consistently applied at the control account level and selected WBS and organizational levels at least monthly as a routine task?

1061. Who are responsible for the establishment of budgets and assignment of resources for overhead performance?

1062. How do you manage changes in the nature of the overhead requirements?

1063. Are there changes in the direct base to which overhead costs are allocated?

1064. How does the monthly budget compare to the actual experience?

1065. Are significant decision points, constraints, and interfaces identified as key milestones?

4.3 Earned Value Status: Collaborative Decision Making

1066. Where is evidence-based earned value in your organization reported?

1067. What is the unit of forecast value?

1068. Validation is a process of ensuring that the developed system will actually achieve the stakeholders desired outcomes; Are you building the right product? What do you validate?

1069. Where are your problem areas?

1070. If earned value management (EVM) is so good in determining the true status of a Collaborative Decision Making project and Collaborative Decision Making project its completion, why is it that hardly any one uses it in information systems related Collaborative Decision Making projects?

1071. Earned value can be used in almost any Collaborative Decision Making project situation and in almost any Collaborative Decision Making project environment. it may be used on large Collaborative Decision Making projects, medium sized Collaborative Decision Making projects, tiny Collaborative Decision Making projects (in cut-down form), complex and simple Collaborative Decision Making projects and in any market sector. some people, of course, know all about earned value, they have used it for years - but perhaps not as effectively as they could have?

1072. Are you hitting your Collaborative Decision Making projects targets?

1073. Verification is a process of ensuring that the developed system satisfies the stakeholders agreements and specifications; Are you building the product right? What do you verify?

1074. How does this compare with other Collaborative Decision Making projects?

1075. When is it going to finish?

1076. How much is it going to cost by the finish?

4.4 Risk Audit: Collaborative Decision Making

1077. Are there any forms the staff is required to sign?

1078. Does the adoption of a business risk audit approach change internal control documentation and testing practices?

1079. Is the auditor able to evaluate contradictory evidence in an unbiased manner?

1080. Is all required equipment available?

1081. Auditor independence: a burdensome constraint or a core value?

1082. Have staff received necessary training?

1083. Who is responsible for what?

1084. The halo effect in business risk audits: can strategic risk assessment bias auditor judgment about accounting details?

1085. Is the customer willing to participate in reviews?

1086. For paid staff, does your organization comply with the minimum conditions for employment and/or the applicable modern award?

1087. Is a software Collaborative Decision Making project management tool available?

1088. Does your organization have any policies or procedures to guide its decision-making (code of conduct for the board, conflict of interest policy, etc.)?

1089. Are enough people available?

1090. Do requirements demand the use of new analysis, design, or testing methods?

1091. Has everyone (staff, volunteers and participants) agreed to a code of behaviour or conduct?

1092. Have you worked with the customer in the past?

1093. Are audit program plans risk-adjusted?

1094. What risk does not having unique identification present?

1095. Are requirements fully understood by the team and customers?

4.5 Contractor Status Report: Collaborative Decision Making

1096. What process manages the contracts?

1097. What is the average response time for answering a support call?

1098. What was the actual budget or estimated cost for your organizations services?

1099. What was the budget or estimated cost for your organizations services?

1100. How long have you been using the services?

1101. How is risk transferred?

1102. Are there contractual transfer concerns?

1103. What was the final actual cost?

1104. Describe how often regular updates are made to the proposed solution. Are corresponding regular updates included in the standard maintenance plan?

1105. If applicable; describe your standard schedule for new software version releases. Are new software version releases included in the standard maintenance plan?

1106. How does the proposed individual meet each requirement?

1107. Who can list a Collaborative Decision Making project as organization experience, your organization or a previous employee of your organization?

1108. What was the overall budget or estimated cost?

1109. What are the minimum and optimal bandwidth requirements for the proposed solution?

4.6 Formal Acceptance: Collaborative Decision Making

1110. Do you buy pre-configured systems or build your own configuration?

1111. General estimate of the costs and times to complete the Collaborative Decision Making project?

1112. What lessons were learned about your Collaborative Decision Making project management methodology?

1113. Was the Collaborative Decision Making project goal achieved?

1114. What function(s) does it fill or meet?

1115. What features, practices, and processes proved to be strengths or weaknesses?

1116. Did the Collaborative Decision Making project manager and team act in a professional and ethical manner?

1117. What are the requirements against which to test, Who will execute?

1118. Does it do what Collaborative Decision Making project team said it would?

1119. Was the client satisfied with the Collaborative Decision Making project results?

1120. Does it do what client said it would?

1121. Do you buy-in installation services?

1122. Was the sponsor/customer satisfied?

1123. Who supplies data?

1124. Who would use it?

1125. What is the Acceptance Management Process?

1126. Is formal acceptance of the Collaborative Decision Making project product documented and distributed?

1127. What can you do better next time?

1128. Was the Collaborative Decision Making project work done on time, within budget, and according to specification?

1129. Have all comments been addressed?

5.0 Closing Process Group: Collaborative Decision Making

1130. Is this a follow-on to a previous Collaborative Decision Making project?

1131. How well did the chosen processes fit the needs of the Collaborative Decision Making project?

1132. Is the Collaborative Decision Making project funded?

1133. Did the Collaborative Decision Making project team have enough people to execute the Collaborative Decision Making project plan?

1134. How will you know you did it?

1135. Can the lesson learned be replicated?

1136. How well defined and documented were the Collaborative Decision Making project management processes you chose to use?

1137. Was the schedule met?

1138. Is there a clear cause and effect between the activity and the lesson learned?

1139. What areas were overlooked on this Collaborative Decision Making project?

1140. Is the Collaborative Decision Making project

funded?

1141. How will you do it?

1142. Based on your Collaborative Decision Making project communication management plan, what worked well?

1143. How dependent is the Collaborative Decision Making project on other Collaborative Decision Making projects or work efforts?

1144. What can you do better next time, and what specific actions can you take to improve?

1145. What is an Encumbrance?

1146. Did the Collaborative Decision Making project management methodology work?

1147. What do you need to do?

1148. What will you do?

5.1 Procurement Audit: Collaborative Decision Making

1149. Relevance of the contract to the Internal Market?

1150. Are budget transfers within the general fund made for only the already stated items permitted by law and regulation?

1151. Are rules in automatic disbursement programs adequate to prevent duplicate payment of invoices?

1152. Are all claims certified by the officer giving rise to the claim (usually the purchasing agent)?

1153. Are there procedures for trade-in arrangements?

1154. Are purchasing actions processed on a timely basis?

1155. Does your organization have an administrative timetable to assist the staff in implementing the budget calendar?

1156. Are regulations on taxes, fees, duties, excises, tariffs etc. not impeding (international) competition?

1157. If information was withheld, was there reasonable justification for this decision?

1158. Are purchase requisitions used to generate

purchase orders?

1159. Are lease-purchase agreements drawn and processed in accordance with law and regulation?

1160. Does the procurement process compile basic procurement information such as how much is bought and spend with individual suppliers?

1161. Is a cash flow chart prepared and used in determining the timing and term of investments?

1162. Were there no material changes in the contract shortly after award?

1163. Is it calculated whether aggregated procurement can be more cost-efficient?

1164. Was the admissibility of variants displayed in the contract notice?

1165. Do all requests for materials, supplies, and services require supervisors authorization?

1166. Has your organization examined in detail the definition of performance?

1167. Were any additional works or deliveries admissible, without recourse to a new procurement procedure?

1168. Does the procurement function/unit have the ability to negotiate with customers and suppliers?

5.2 Contract Close-Out: Collaborative Decision Making

1169. Was the contract type appropriate?

1170. Change in circumstances?

1171. Have all acceptance criteria been met prior to final payment to contractors?

1172. Parties: who is involved?

1173. Was the contract complete without requiring numerous changes and revisions?

1174. Was the contract sufficiently clear so as not to result in numerous disputes and misunderstandings?

1175. Have all contracts been closed?

1176. Parties: Authorized?

1177. Have all contract records been included in the Collaborative Decision Making project archives?

1178. What happens to the recipient of services?

1179. How does it work?

1180. Why Outsource?

1181. Are the signers the authorized officials?

1182. Have all contracts been completed?

1183. What is capture management?

1184. Change in knowledge?

1185. How/when used ?

1186. Change in attitude or behavior?

1187. Has each contract been audited to verify acceptance and delivery?

1188. How is the contracting office notified of the automatic contract close-out?

5.3 Project or Phase Close-Out: Collaborative Decision Making

1189. Who controlled key decisions that were made?

1190. What are they?

1191. What security considerations needed to be addressed during the procurement life cycle?

1192. What process was planned for managing issues/risks?

1193. Was the user/client satisfied with the end product?

1194. Were cost budgets met?

1195. What hierarchical authority does the stakeholder have in your organization?

1196. Does the lesson describe a function that would be done differently the next time?

1197. Which changes might a stakeholder be required to make as a result of the Collaborative Decision Making project?

1198. Who controlled the resources for the Collaborative Decision Making project?

1199. Is the lesson based on actual Collaborative Decision Making project experience rather than on independent research?

1200. What were the actual outcomes?

1201. What are the marketing communication needs for each stakeholder?

1202. Is the lesson significant, valid, and applicable?

1203. What could have been improved?

1204. Does the lesson educate others to improve performance?

1205. Planned remaining costs?

5.4 Lessons Learned: Collaborative Decision Making

1206. How mature are the observations?

1207. How well does the product or service the Collaborative Decision Making project produced meet the defined Collaborative Decision Making project requirements?

1208. Was sufficient time allocated to review Collaborative Decision Making project deliverables?

1209. How well prepared were you to receive Collaborative Decision Making project deliverables?

1210. What were the main bottlenecks on the process?

1211. What specialization does the task require?

1212. Will the information remain current?

1213. What other questions should you have asked?

1214. Why does your organization need a lessons learned (LL) capability?

1215. How spontaneous are the communications?

1216. What are the internal dependencies?

1217. How useful and complete was the Collaborative

Decision Making project document repository?

1218. What is your overall assessment of the outcome of this Collaborative Decision Making project?

1219. Was sufficient advance training conducted and/or information provided to enable the already stated affected by the changes to adjust to and accommodate them?

1220. How effectively and timely was your organizational change impact identified and planned for?

1221. What is your organizations performance history?

1222. What are the skills directly related to the task?

1223. What is the distribution of authority?

1224. How effectively were issues managed on the Collaborative Decision Making project?

Index

ability 37, 82, 202, 258
absences   233
absent 234
acceptable   51, 89, 97, 146, 195, 237
acceptance   9, 112, 223, 228, 253-254, 259-260
accepted   105, 142, 153, 185
accepting   161
access 4, 10-12, 25, 143, 146, 185, 197, 212, 233, 239
accomplish   10, 80, 112, 125, 134, 218, 236
accordance   258
according   35, 37, 158, 160, 203, 254
account   37, 59, 158, 173, 203, 230, 246
accounted   177
accounting   193, 249
accounts   193
accuracy   152, 211
accurate   12, 118, 128, 164
achievable   119
achieve   10, 65, 85, 89, 108, 123, 131, 164, 189, 191-192, 203, 209, 237, 241, 247
achieved   28, 79, 83, 121, 196, 229, 253
achieving   204, 227
acquire   221
acquired   162
across 59, 142, 188
action 56, 96-97, 102-103, 139, 143, 152, 158, 187, 203, 230
actionable   56, 126
actions 28, 57, 99, 104, 127, 137, 161, 182, 191, 204, 232, 245, 256-257
active 136
activities   19, 21, 24, 33, 80, 95, 123, 162-163, 165-166, 168, 171, 173, 175, 177, 180-181, 196, 201, 203, 209, 229-230
activity 5-6, 32, 36, 80, 144, 162-166, 168, 170, 173-174, 176, 178-179, 181-182, 188, 219, 232, 255
actors 136
actual 36, 47, 146, 193, 246, 251, 261-262
actually   38, 64, 87, 103, 188, 190, 205, 247
adaptive   238
addition   114
additional   40, 43, 64, 160, 173, 184, 207, 232, 258

additions	102
address	1, 26, 133, 137, 178, 191, 224
addressed	170, 223, 254, 261
addressing	37
adequate	32, 141, 151, 153, 157, 180, 215, 237, 257
adequately	43, 177, 179, 194, 231
adjust	100-101, 264
adjusted	96
admissible	258
adopted	139
adoption	249
advance	233, 264
advancing	229
advantage	1, 65, 118, 190
advantages	114, 148, 166
adverse	245
advise	2
affect	72-73, 89, 115, 129, 132, 149, 151, 174, 185, 203-204, 213, 216, 223, 225, 235-236
affected	198, 210-211, 217, 223, 264
affecting	14, 28, 75, 139
afford	204
affordable	89
against	37, 94, 100, 152, 158, 230, 235, 253
agenda	233-234
agendas	125
aggregate	59
aggregated	258
agreed	198, 211, 250
Agreement	8, 118, 233
agreements	62, 82, 85, 160, 248, 258
agrees	113
aiming	108
alerts	98
aligned	22
alignment	138
alleged	3
allocate	116, 181, 245
allocated	48, 58, 108, 246, 263
allocating	245
allowable	51
allowed	2, 120, 171
allows	12, 169

almost 247
already 123, 160, 187, 189, 221, 257, 264
always 12
ambitious 237
amount 24, 144
amplify 71, 107
analysing 208
analysis 4, 8, 12-13, 60, 64-65, 69, 73, 90, 136, 142, 145, 172, 179, 183, 185-186, 189, 193, 206, 209, 213, 224, 245-246, 250
analyze 4, 60, 74, 207
analyzed 98, 179, 209
annually 158
another 155
anothers 235
answer 13-14, 18, 30, 46, 60, 76, 93, 105, 223
answered 29, 45, 59, 75, 91, 104, 129
answering 13, 166, 251
anyone 41, 128
anything 164, 170, 190, 228
appear 3, 219
applicable 13, 103, 157-158, 228, 249, 251, 262
applied 81, 97, 138, 245-246
appointed 33, 44
appraise 137
appreciate 195
approach 80, 91, 114, 129, 153, 161, 221, 235, 243-244, 249
approaches 83
approval 37, 109, 233
approvals 145, 154
approve 224
approved 36, 63, 131, 142, 145, 149, 151, 161, 186, 223, 225
approving 149
Architects 10
archives 259
arising 132
around 106, 118
articulate 244
artifact 235
ascertain 158
ascribed 205
asking 3, 10, 191-192
aspects 166, 212, 214
assess 19, 104, 111

assessed 203
assessing 83, 98
assessment 7-8, 11-12, 23, 145, 160, 180, 195, 201, 205, 235, 237, 249, 264
assets 51
assign 22
assigned 141, 152, 155, 158, 215, 218, 231, 246
assigning 171
assignment 6, 164, 193, 246
assist 11, 74, 96, 183, 219, 227, 257
assistant 10
assume 237
assuming 206
Assumption 5, 153
assurance 24, 128, 144, 151, 161
attached 176
attainable 32
attempted 41
attempting 95
attend 22
attendance 44
attended 1, 44
attention 14, 127
attitude 260
attitudes 89, 222
attributes 5, 109, 164, 223-224
audited 211, 260
auditing 19, 96
auditor 249
audits 215, 249
author 3
authority 158, 196, 202, 261, 264
authorize 223
authorized 141, 157, 194, 246, 259
authors 187
automatic 257, 260
available 25, 27, 43, 53, 71, 77, 96, 109, 142, 157, 162-163, 168, 173, 177, 189, 204-206, 218, 228, 237-238, 241, 249-250
Average 14, 29, 45, 59, 75, 91, 104, 129, 197, 228, 251
avoided 205
awareness 69, 136
background 12, 133, 166
backup 152

backward 225
balance 196
balanced 77
bandwidth 252
barriers 115, 134
baseline 6, 127, 137, 141, 152, 157, 185-186
baselined 211
baselines 43
basics 117
because 2, 177
become 108-109, 123-124, 145-146, 149, 227
becomes 202
before 1-2, 12, 41, 99, 143, 162, 168, 176, 185, 201, 211, 223-224
beginning 4, 17, 29, 45, 59, 75, 92, 104, 129
behavior 243, 260
behaviors 26, 195, 227, 244
behaviour 250
behind 2
belief 13, 18, 30, 46, 60, 76, 93, 105-106
believable 119
believe 2, 106, 113
benchmark 189
benefit 3, 22, 25, 47, 103, 174
benefits 24, 50, 58-59, 68, 105, 115-116, 121, 124, 133, 154, 168
better 10, 35, 55, 85, 102, 137, 162, 174-175, 183, 208, 210, 232, 236, 254, 256
between 139, 149, 161, 187, 215, 224, 255
biased 207
biggest 57, 81, 181
blinding 66
bother 52
bought 258
bounce 70
boundaries 36
bounds 36
Breakdown 5-6, 139, 155, 171
briefed 33
brings 34
broken 62
broker 179
budget 2, 94-95, 109, 138, 141, 143-144, 157, 176, 211, 246, 251-252, 254, 257

budgeted 47, 159, 245
budgets 26, 123, 157-158, 245-246, 261
building 28, 97, 247-248
burdensome 249
business 2, 10, 12, 23, 26, 34, 47, 55-56, 63, 74, 83, 86, 91, 104, 107-108, 110, 113, 119, 121, 123, 126, 131, 134, 145, 147, 194, 215, 217, 225, 245, 249
buy-in 254
buyout 141
calculated 258
calendar 257
calendars 160
cannot 169
capability 19, 154, 180, 185, 263
capable 10, 39
capacities 121
capacity 19, 28, 82
capital 127
capitalize 67
capture 56, 100, 260
captured 47, 72, 89, 118, 143-144, 179
capturing 228
career 149
careers 118
carried 63, 198, 209
catching 1
categories 206
category 42
caused 3, 50
causes 47, 51, 60, 66-67, 71, 99, 141, 173
causing 28, 216
celebrate 78
center 51
central 228
centrally 77
certain 131, 201
certified 179, 257
challenge 10, 228
challenges 125, 167
champions 192
chance 209
chances 201

change   7-8, 18, 22, 44, 47, 50, 63, 67-68, 78, 81, 89, 91, 100, 112, 133, 135, 141, 145-146, 155, 161, 165, 169, 173-174, 181, 185, 188, 202, 213, 217-218, 223-226, 239, 241, 249, 259-260, 264
changed   27, 44, 88, 95, 123, 132, 148, 183, 217, 224
changes   32, 44, 63, 79, 88, 99, 102, 111-112, 126, 133, 144, 146, 151-153, 157, 173, 185-186, 194, 198, 211, 223-224, 226, 232, 237, 246, 258-259, 261, 264
changing   100, 118
charged   194
charter 4, 34-35, 87, 133-134, 161, 180, 197, 215
charts 65, 178
cheaper   55
checked   68, 96, 101, 103, 148
checklists   11
choice 42, 125
choose   13
choosing   205
chosen 134, 219, 241-242, 255
circumvent   18
claimed   3
claims 189, 257
clarify 116
classes 174, 198
classified   158
clearly 13, 18, 25, 30, 38, 42, 46, 60, 75-76, 88, 93, 105, 148, 195-196, 198, 215, 243
client   51, 131, 209, 253-254, 261
clients 25, 42, 242
closed 101, 193, 225, 259
closely 12
Close-Out   9, 259-261
closest 111
Closing 9, 255
coaches   31, 191
coherent   160
coherently   230
colleague   120
colleagues   112, 119, 175
collect 73, 103, 183, 191, 232
collected   35, 39, 62, 69, 71-72
collection   65
combine   83
coming   61

command 97
comments 254
commit 160, 243
commitment 104, 116, 214
committed 64, 154, 187, 198, 201
Committee 187
common 152, 177, 181, 212-213
community 176, 183-184, 210, 229
companies 3, 96
company 1-2, 10, 55, 65, 107, 109, 113, 118, 120, 127
compare 61, 80, 246, 248
compared 113
comparison 13
compatible 225, 243
compelling 33
competing 55
competitor 2
compile 258
complaints 189
complete 3, 11, 13, 24, 31, 40, 43, 128, 141, 163, 165, 167, 169, 173, 189, 201, 253, 259, 263
completed 14, 30, 38, 41, 44, 131, 143, 162, 168, 201, 232, 260
completely 1, 175, 205
completing 106, 168
completion 32-33, 139, 158, 169, 182, 193-194, 243, 247
complex 10, 115, 142, 247
complexity 22, 49, 63, 80
compliance 1, 28, 49, 61, 82, 154, 238
comply 249
component 187
components 153, 158, 161
compute 14
computer 154
concept 80, 191
concerned 21
concerns 2, 21, 25, 111, 251
concrete 83, 236, 243
condition 94, 177, 187
conditions 103, 114, 173, 232, 249
conduct 250
conducted 160, 180, 186, 189, 197, 212, 215, 264
confidence 190, 205, 207

confirm	13
Conflict	199, 233, 250
conflicts	232-233
conform	154
connected	177
connecting	109
consensus	234
consider	18-19, 28, 213
considered	25, 57, 227-228
considers	65
consistent	42, 56, 100, 194, 205, 229, 244-245
constantly	1, 199
Constraint	5, 153, 249
consult	1
consultant	1-2, 10, 181
consulted	119
consulting	2, 50
consumers	123
Contact	10
contacts	122, 217
contain	20, 62, 101
contained	3, 193
contains	11
content	33, 141, 223, 228
contents	3-4, 11
context	31, 35, 40
continual	95, 101
continuing	230
Continuity	55, 166
continuous	62, 81
contract	9, 157-158, 160, 173, 197, 221, 231-232, 238, 245, 257-260
contractor	8, 145, 152, 157, 251
contracts	37, 62, 179, 220, 251, 259-260
contribute	136
control	4, 33, 53, 61, 93-94, 97, 99-100, 102-103, 145-146, 158, 173, 184, 193, 223-224, 245-246, 249
controlled	65, 202, 239, 261
controls	20, 68, 71, 76, 86-87, 93, 97-98, 100-101
convention	115
converge	243
convey	3
cooperate	183

coordinate 212
Copyright 3
corporate 2
correct 46, 93
corrective 57, 99, 158, 161, 204, 230
correspond 11-12, 158
costing 53
counting 119
counts 119
course 44, 50, 247
covering 11, 100
crashing 168
craziest 110
create 69, 107, 114, 189
created 71, 75, 95, 135, 138-139, 141, 198, 209, 219
creating 10, 57, 216
creative 26
creativity 81
credible 183
crisis 19
criteria 4, 7, 11-12, 32, 42-43, 63, 85, 98, 107, 124, 130-131, 137, 149, 180, 183, 198, 213, 217, 259
CRITERION 4, 18, 30, 46, 60, 76, 93, 105, 143
critical 32-33, 35, 72, 91, 96, 101, 124, 173, 205, 213, 220, 227, 238, 245
criticism 75, 235
criticized 236
crucial 61, 166
crystal 13
culture 44, 75, 143, 161, 190, 195-196
current 32, 46, 55, 61-63, 83, 88, 94, 106, 111, 114, 122, 126, 157, 174, 187, 203, 263
currently 35, 228, 237
custom 27
customer 19, 33-35, 37-39, 89, 99, 101, 107, 111, 116, 120, 124, 133, 147-148, 151, 201, 205, 208, 223-224, 245, 249-250, 254
customers 3, 19, 38-39, 55-56, 58, 61, 63, 102, 106, 108, 110-111, 115, 119, 121, 124, 126-127, 147, 188, 209, 222, 245, 250, 258
customized 2
cut-down 247
cycles 133
damage 3, 207
Dashboard 11

dashboards 102
day-to-day 95, 109
deadlines 25, 112, 136
decide 87, 196, 220
decider 86
deciding 107
Decision 3-9, 11-16, 18-45, 47-92, 94-133, 135-139, 141-149, 151-158, 160-181, 183-187, 189-191, 193-199, 201-209, 211-213, 215-217, 219-223, 225-229, 231, 233-237, 239-243, 245-249, 251-257, 259, 261, 263-264
decisions 78-79, 82-83, 87, 90-91, 102, 104, 211, 227-228, 231-233, 261
dedicated 10
deeper 13
defect 190, 198, 230
defects 131
define 4, 30, 40-41, 44, 69, 74, 152, 155, 174-175, 227
defined 13, 18, 20, 30-32, 35, 37-39, 41-43, 46, 60, 65, 74, 76, 93, 105, 151, 153, 155, 157, 165, 173, 195-196, 198, 215, 220, 255, 263
defines 24, 37, 44, 171
defining 10, 120, 154
definite 101, 165
definition 25, 27, 40-43, 154, 191, 198, 258
degree 207, 235-238, 243-244
-degree 2
delaying 56
delays 52, 163, 177
delegate 234
delegated 39
delete 181
deletions 102
deliver 19, 32, 89, 115, 121, 183
delivered 49, 124, 185, 231
deliveries 258
delivers 171
delivery 23, 57, 114, 126, 167, 260
demand 250
demands 243
department 10, 107, 197, 221
depend 222
dependent 126, 256
depends 127

depict 169
deploy 102, 127
deployed 98
deploying 50, 91
deployment 48, 230
derive 98
describe 23, 133, 149, 251, 261
described 3, 147, 226
describing 38
deserving 222
design 12, 62, 66, 84, 97, 129, 206, 250
designed 10, 12, 64, 89
designing 10
desired 26, 43, 70, 83, 225, 247
detail 133, 151-152, 155, 164, 176, 230, 258
detailed 71, 75, 138, 145, 160
details 49, 218, 249
detect 103, 189
determine 12, 112, 129, 162, 174, 183, 219, 238
determined 65, 129, 173, 191-192
detracting 126
develop 55, 76-77, 79, 82, 87, 142, 145, 155, 243
developed 12, 34, 39, 44, 47, 87, 144, 152-154, 158, 161, 191, 197, 225, 247-248
developer 208
developers 224
developing 63, 77, 215
develops 238
diagnose 207
diagnostic 209
diagram 6, 49, 56, 66, 168-169
diagrams 52
dictates 177
Dictionary 5, 157
differ 178
difference 139, 227
different 10, 25, 37-39, 66, 74, 125, 129, 187, 205, 207-208
difficult 69, 162, 165-166, 168, 171, 173, 179
dilemma 114
dimensions 26
direct 245-246
direction 44, 55, 141
directions 210

directly 3, 61, 63, 199, 264
Directory 8, 231
Disagree 13, 18, 30, 46, 60, 76, 93, 105
disaster 55, 57, 177
disclosed 214
disclosure 96, 158
discover 145
discussion 109
displayed 35, 62, 162, 175, 258
disputes 233, 259
disqualify 64
disruptive 63
distribute 232
Divided 28, 39, 44, 59, 75, 91, 104, 129
document 12, 144-147, 153, 227, 232, 264
documented 35, 78, 88, 94, 98, 101-102, 132, 151, 153-154, 161, 186, 195, 220, 223, 246, 254-255
documents 10, 177, 187
domains 87
dormant 122
drawback 215
Driver 74
drivers 53, 74
drives 53
driving 110, 116
duplicate 257
Duration 6, 156-157, 173, 175
durations 36, 160, 220
during 44, 80, 132, 170, 190, 206, 209, 228, 261
duties 257
dynamics 36
eagerly 2
earlier 120
earliest 146
earned 8, 179, 193, 247
economic 210
economical 128, 141
economy 82, 174
edition 11
editorial 3
educate 262
educated 1
education 27, 101, 230

effect 249, 255
effective 21, 106, 112, 128, 147, 158, 175, 188, 209, 214-215, 228-230
effects 51, 136, 166, 204
efficiency 70
efficient 57, 87, 139, 222
effort 31, 52, 56, 58, 113, 142, 146, 157, 161, 241
efforts 41, 86, 143, 256
Electrical 153
electronic 3
element 157
elements 12, 34, 67, 80, 99, 129, 133, 151, 160-161, 180, 192-193, 246
embarking 33
embeddings 189
emerging 1, 64, 101
emphasis 227
employed 212
employee 87, 124, 187, 252
employees 25-26, 28, 66, 115, 119, 121, 237
employers 135
employment 249
empower 10
enable 63, 69, 264
enablers 121
encourage 81, 236
end-users 207
energy 1
engage 114, 234-235, 244
engagement 56, 135, 199, 233
engages 229
Engineers 153
enhance 101
enhanced 118, 230
enhancing 95
enough 10, 63, 119, 127, 129, 131, 150, 215, 236, 242, 250, 255
ensure 36-37, 62, 67, 106, 111-112, 114, 153, 180, 187, 189, 197, 215, 219, 229, 232, 236
ensures 114
ensuring 12, 108, 247-248
Enterprise 221
entire 189

entities 49, 142, 230
entity   3, 238
entrance   229
equipment   20, 23, 229, 249
equitably   39, 236
errors   107, 131, 181
escalated   219
Escalation   180
essential   82, 236
essentials   125
establish   76, 102, 184, 208
estimate   49, 51, 57, 141, 178, 207, 253
-estimate   182
estimated   32-33, 57, 106, 181, 183-184, 207, 251-252
estimates   6, 34, 54, 63, 144, 173, 178-179, 181, 186, 194
Estimating   6, 143, 160, 175, 183-184
estimation   82, 212
etcetera   49, 114
ethical 26, 118, 253
ethnic 107
evaluate   81, 84, 89, 197, 249
evaluated   173, 214
evaluating   85
evaluation   63, 77, 86, 99, 157, 213, 235, 238
evaluators   213, 239
events 22, 85, 174
everyday   1, 66
everyone   39-40, 151, 190, 229, 234, 250
everything   47
evidence   13, 48, 203, 221, 249
evident   215
evolution   46
exactly 195, 229
examined   42, 258
example   4, 11, 15, 23, 68, 104, 153, 158
examples   10-11, 134
exceed   156
exceeding   56
excellence   10, 42
excellent   57
exception   237
excises 257
excited   1

exciting	243
exclude	79
excluded	157
execute	131, 242, 253, 255
executed	185, 226
Executing	7, 154, 199, 219
execution	102, 154, 224, 231
executive	10, 107, 133, 212
executives	124
existence	205
existing	12, 104, 120, 151
expect	112
expected	24, 36, 78, 108, 112, 138, 141, 182, 241, 245
expend	56
expenses	245
experience	36, 111, 125, 129, 166, 175, 194, 196, 202, 230, 246, 252, 261
expertise	83, 142, 144
experts	32
explained	12
explicit	191
explicitly	123
explore	66
explored	205
extensive	2
extent	13, 21-22, 43, 78, 139
external	1-2, 41, 105, 193
facilitate	13, 23, 69-70, 77, 102, 243
facing	18, 114
fact-based	244
factored	136
factors	52, 79, 126, 133, 183
failed	49
failing	203
failure	47, 112, 124, 209
fairly	39
familiar	11
fashion	3
feasible	51, 65, 121, 184, 201
feature	12
features	142, 253
feedback	33, 39, 49
feeling	1

fields   136
finalized   15
financial   58, 62-63, 68, 115-116, 136, 204, 241
fingertips   12
finish   133, 146, 162, 166-167, 248
finished   133, 166
focuses   131
follow 94, 120, 168
followed   32, 143
following   11, 13
follow-on   255
for--and   100
forecast   197, 247
forecasts   158, 179
forefront   125
foresee   167
foreseen   132
forever 123, 187
forget   12
formal 9, 115, 197, 215, 217, 243-244, 253-254
formally   42, 160, 179, 194, 201
format 12, 223
formats   203
formula   14, 108
Formulate   30
forward   2, 110, 117
foster   108, 127, 195
framework   97, 126, 191-192
freaky   119
frequency   43, 96, 185, 190, 209
frequent   211
frequently   54, 233, 236
friend   114, 117, 120
friends 2, 236
frontiers   90
fulfill   120, 131
full-blown   53
full-scale   84
function   242, 253, 258, 261
functional   141, 157-158, 238
functions   31, 72, 111, 128, 147, 171, 196, 243
funded255-256
funding   119, 129, 131

further 11, 204
future   10, 55, 97, 100, 102, 109, 245
gained 2, 94, 97
gather 13, 31, 34-36, 38-39, 41, 43, 46, 67-68, 73
gathered   38, 63, 66, 70-71, 73-74
gathering   40, 43, 147
general   80, 164, 253, 257
generally   222
generate   64, 71, 257
generated   75, 194
generation   11, 72
generic   2
geographic   137
gestation   206
getting 2, 54, 227
giving   257
Global 82, 166
govern 120
governance   19, 120, 230, 237
granted   185
graphical   178
graphics   25
graphs 11
greatest   81
ground 68
grouped   164
groups 129, 154, 172, 187, 198, 211, 221
growth 66, 126
guarantee   80
guidelines   214, 227
guiding   230
handle 170, 232-233
handled   158, 234
happen   20, 127, 167, 203, 209, 217, 223
happened   223
happens   10, 32, 52, 56, 110, 124, 129, 183, 209, 259
hardest   57
hardly 247
hardware   154, 173
Havent 113, 201
having 234, 250
hazards   209
health 110, 202

hearing 107
helping 10, 152, 241
hidden 52
higher 190
highest 28
high-level 30, 41
highlight 2
high-tech 123
hijacking 119
hinder 195
hindrance 230
hiring 102
historical 183
history 162, 264
hitters 65
hitting 248
holiday 2
honest 118
Honestly 2
horizon 116
humans 10
hypotheses 60
identified 3, 22, 24, 27, 37-38, 73, 75, 80, 84, 132, 139, 153, 157-158, 160-161, 164, 173, 179-180, 186, 189, 193-195, 203, 205-206, 212, 215, 227, 246, 264
identify 1, 12-13, 23, 27, 64, 68, 158, 183, 193, 207
ignore 21
ignoring 124
imbedded 97
immediate 204
impact 7, 41, 49, 51-52, 54-57, 110, 132, 148, 182, 186, 201, 203-205, 207, 213, 219, 226, 236-237, 239, 264
impacted 48, 154
impacts 48, 137, 154, 175, 203
impeding 257
implement 28, 56, 62, 93
implicit 127
importance 213, 235
important 19, 21, 42, 61, 63, 108, 116, 118, 121-122, 128, 139, 171, 194, 199, 219, 234, 243
improve 4, 12, 74, 76, 80-90, 131, 133, 153, 171, 188, 190, 232, 237, 256, 262
improved 2, 81, 85, 87, 90, 95, 137, 214, 262

improves	132
improving	84, 222
inactive	181
inadequate	1
incentives	102, 238
incident	228
include	26, 79, 83, 137, 163, 180, 213-214, 223, 245
included	4, 10, 21, 47, 61, 147-148, 158, 175-176, 183, 214, 216, 251, 259
INCLUDES	12
including	19, 31, 35, 40, 50, 58, 70, 97, 99, 103, 154
in-coming	187
increase	78, 118
increased	115
increasing	108, 227
incurred	51
incurring	158, 194
in-depth	11, 13
indicate	64, 94, 124
indicated	99
indicators	27, 50, 58, 61, 63, 66, 83, 97, 157, 201, 207
indirect	158, 181, 194, 245
indirectly	3
individual	58, 162, 188, 234, 243-244, 251, 258
industry	1-2, 95, 113, 122
influence	90, 118, 135, 196, 200, 227-228
influences	166
inform	236
informal	217, 243-244
informed	131, 137, 193
ingrained	100
inherent	111, 195
in-house	2
initial	36, 107, 133
initially	42
initiate	158
initiated	184, 225
Initiating	4, 112, 131
initiative	13, 136, 188, 191-192, 199, 240
Innovate	76
innovation	47, 65, 70, 82, 99, 127, 129, 167, 188
innovative	114, 139, 183, 242
in-process	61

inputs 37-38, 59, 71, 96
inside 24
insight 64
insights 1-2, 11
inspect 224
inspector 224
inspired 121
Instead 2, 122, 174
Institute 153
insure 117
integral 189
integrate 88, 103, 117, 142
integrated 132
integrity 28, 113, 226
intended 3, 85
INTENT 18, 30, 46, 60, 76, 93, 105
intention 3
intentions 230
intents 138
interact 111
interest 122, 221, 250
interested 137
interests 24, 136
interfaces 246
interim 112
internal 1, 3, 41, 64, 105, 125, 157, 166, 249, 257, 263
interpret 13
intervals 212
interview 1, 117
introduce 205
introduced 236
inventory 181
invest 74
investing 2
investment 21, 56, 64, 187
invoices 211, 257
involve 123
involved 19, 21, 37, 72-73, 77, 106, 137-138, 144, 154, 160, 187, 196-197, 215, 220-221, 235, 259
involves 98
issues 18, 20-21, 23-25, 28, 131-132, 151-152, 170, 211, 215, 219, 230-231, 261, 264
iterative 147

itself   3, 21
jointly   236
judgment   249
justified 99, 131
killer   114
knock-on   204
knowledge   1-2, 12, 31, 36, 41, 83, 85, 93-94, 97, 101-103, 108, 113, 117, 125, 188, 193, 196, 233, 260
lacked 95
largely 62
latest   11
leader 70, 75, 83, 205
leaders 40, 73, 104, 109, 127
leadership   35, 41, 82, 110, 127
learned   1, 9, 100, 118, 192, 212, 253, 255, 263
learning   99, 101, 103, 228, 230
lesson   255, 261-262
lessons 9, 84, 100, 118, 192, 212, 253, 263
letter   214
Leveling   164
levels   19, 28, 37, 61, 63, 83, 95, 97, 110, 155, 187, 246
leverage   34, 82, 100, 111, 183, 233
leveraged   41
liability 3
licensed   3
lifecycle   189
lifecycles   83
Lifetime   12
likelihood   85, 203
likely   84, 94, 120, 186, 228
limitation   57
limited 12
linear   147
Linked 42, 227
listed   177, 180, 192
listen   106, 126, 234
little   2
locally 77, 179
located   179
location   228, 233
logical 170
longer 1, 97
long-term   94, 121, 125

looked 1
looking 20, 182
losses   25, 41
lowest 169
magnitude   88
maintain   93, 113, 126
maintained   79, 194, 229, 244
majority   234
makers 77, 103, 241
Making 3-9, 11-16, 18-45, 47-92, 94-133, 135-139, 141-149, 151-158, 160-181, 183-187, 189-191, 193-199, 201-209, 211-213, 215-217, 219-227, 229, 231, 233-237, 239-243, 245, 247-249, 251-257, 259, 261, 263-264
manage   31, 34, 48, 51, 55, 62, 74, 77, 83, 85-86, 89, 111, 113, 133, 141, 149, 173, 181, 188, 191, 197, 239, 246
manageable   40, 89, 161
managed   10, 72, 74, 77, 86, 91, 97, 100, 143, 145, 264
management 5-7, 11-12, 19, 21, 25, 31, 35, 46, 64, 66-67, 72, 77-79, 81-82, 85, 87-88, 108, 111, 113, 125, 138-139, 141-143, 145, 153, 157-158, 160-161, 165, 172-175, 179-181, 185, 187-188, 193-194, 197-203, 206-207, 211, 215, 217, 220-221, 224, 233, 242, 245, 247, 249, 253-256, 260
manager   10, 12, 27, 32, 37, 117, 133, 160, 180, 221, 253
managers   4, 130, 158, 201, 219
manages   81-82, 251
managing   4, 78, 130, 135-136, 178, 202, 230, 261
mandatory   225
manner   25, 82, 158, 188, 194, 211, 223, 249, 253
mantle 109
mapping   66, 72-73, 220
market 23, 167, 174, 247, 257
marketer   10
marketing   123, 136, 188, 262
markets   20
Master 178
material   167, 187, 193, 258
materials   3, 233, 258
matrices   149
Matrix 4-7, 136, 149, 193, 207
matter 32, 50, 58
matters   228
mature 193, 263
maximizing   119, 174

meaning 165
meaningful 53, 109
measurable 32, 34, 182, 230, 243
measure 4, 12, 19, 21, 34, 43, 46, 48-50, 53, 55-58, 61, 70, 76, 78, 84-87, 94-95, 104, 152, 183, 235
measured 23, 47-51, 57, 59, 83, 94, 96, 209
measures 50, 53-55, 58-59, 61, 63, 70, 72, 83, 94-95, 97, 139, 187, 191, 204, 210, 236, 238, 242
measuring 95, 245
mechanical 3
mechanism 202
mechanisms 139
mediated 233
medium 247
meeting 37, 43, 101, 185, 188, 191, 199, 222, 228, 231, 233-234
meetings 36, 38, 44, 152, 219, 227, 241
megatrends 107
member 8, 35, 110, 127, 172, 194, 200, 214, 221, 233-234, 237
members 1, 31, 39, 67, 96, 144, 151-152, 160, 177, 179, 199, 216, 232-236, 243-244
membership 237
memorable 189
mentors 205
merely 137
message 95
messages 199
method 52, 142, 152, 164, 175, 189, 199, 208, 234-236
methods 33, 43, 51, 68, 154, 183, 206, 212, 250
metrics 6, 39, 73, 102, 179, 189, 197
milestone 5, 166, 174, 180, 215
milestones 35, 135, 157-158, 246
minimise 217
minimize 157, 201, 219
minimizing 119
minimum 249, 252
minority 24
minutes 43, 91, 231, 234
missed 53, 107
missing 70, 114, 164
mission 65, 73, 111, 122, 210, 229-230, 243
mitigated 2, 202, 208

mitigating 161
mitigation 136, 141-142, 205, 207
modeling 62
models 23, 47, 117
modern 249
modified 102, 223
module 146
moment 107
moments 61
momentum 107
Monday 1
monetary 25
monitor 94-96, 98, 161, 183, 212, 242
monitored 97-98, 102, 132, 174, 176
monitoring 8, 95, 99-100, 102, 170, 207, 215, 241
monthly 246
months 1, 81, 91
morning 1
motivate 122, 243
motivated 197
motivation 25, 98, 133
motive 191-192
moving 117
multiple 61, 187, 207, 212, 229, 239
mutual 138
narrative 166, 188
narrow 67
national 138, 210
nature 246
nearest 14
nearly 113
necessary 62, 67, 72, 114, 117, 126, 139, 154, 157, 183, 219, 226, 231, 237, 241, 249
needed 2, 20, 23, 25, 27-28, 37, 61, 65, 69, 71, 93, 97, 99, 134, 173, 175, 181-182, 191, 199, 217, 239, 241, 261
negative 111, 178, 217
negatively 204
negotiate 258
negotiated 118
neither 3
network 6, 168-169, 217
networks 88
Neutral 13, 18, 30, 46, 60, 76, 93, 105

nonlinear 189
normal 100, 220
notice 3, 258
notified 199, 201, 217, 260
number 28, 44, 53, 59, 75, 91, 104, 129, 165, 172, 265
numbers 115
numerous 259
objection 20-21
objective 10, 49, 132, 157, 205, 227
objectives 2, 19, 22, 28, 30, 42, 65, 73, 98, 103, 112, 115, 124, 128, 136, 154, 177, 179, 187, 197, 204, 209, 222, 238, 243
observe 195
observing 154
obsolete 107
obstacles 18, 183
obtain 126, 173
obtained 39, 154
obtaining 59
obviously 13
occurrence 201
occurring 132, 206
occurs 19, 57, 99, 139, 173, 220, 230
offerings 61, 81
offeror 213
office 131, 143, 221, 260
officer 1, 257
officials 259
one-time 10
ongoing 79, 96, 176
on-going 161, 212
on-site 232
opened 193
operate 210
operates 122
operating 8, 50, 59, 100, 233
operation 99, 175, 185
operations 12, 91, 95, 100, 102-103, 185
operators 94, 190
opponent 228
opposite 106, 122
opposition 108
optimal 87, 252
optimize 78, 90, 95

optimized 116, 143
option 125, 238
options 27, 204
ordered 1
orders 181, 258
organize 142
organized 164
orient 101
origin 148
original 143, 157, 201, 227
originate 103, 200
others 132, 177, 183-184, 194, 199-200, 206, 208, 243, 262
otherwise 3, 158
outcome 13, 80, 136, 264
outcomes 90, 95, 123, 183, 247, 262
outlined 98
output 34, 63, 67-70, 74-75, 94, 103
outputs 38, 66, 71, 73, 96, 151, 170
outside 81, 229, 234, 241
outsource 68, 220, 259
outweigh 59
overall 12-13, 22, 53, 103, 110, 126, 154, 177, 213, 242, 252, 264
overcome 183
overhead 158, 194, 245-246
overlook 200
overlooked 211, 255
oversees 132
oversight 72, 143, 152
overtime 164
owners 155
ownership 38, 93, 138
package 159
packages 157
paradigms 111
paragraph 119
parallel 169
parameters 96, 143
paramount 201
Pareto 65
parking 234
particular 68
Parties 2, 259
partners 19, 37, 96, 115, 127, 235

pattern 164
patterns 82
paying 127
payment 211, 257, 259
payments 160
pending 225
people 10, 22, 49, 57, 61, 74-75, 77, 86, 104, 106, 108, 110-111, 114, 118, 122-123, 127, 131, 153, 197, 207, 210, 216, 222, 242, 247, 250, 255
perceive 114
perceived 207
percent 120
percentage 149
perception 81, 87, 118, 189
perform 22, 37, 39, 142, 145, 163, 171, 188, 236
performed 79, 144, 149, 159, 162-163
performers 197
performing 174, 230, 237
perhaps 27, 247
period 89, 193, 206
permission 3
permit 157
permitted 257
person 3, 20, 136, 194, 199
personal 118
personally 149
personnel 25, 66, 98, 144, 169, 180, 191-192, 215, 230
pertinent 98
phases 80, 199
pitfalls 111
planet 104
planned 97-98, 146, 164, 174, 179, 204, 261-262, 264
planners 103
planning 5, 11, 96, 99, 102, 132-133, 138-139, 142, 158, 169-170, 221
players 87
playing 2
pocket 184
pockets 184
points 28, 44, 59, 67, 75, 91, 104, 129, 246
policies 142, 196, 217, 250
policy 42, 83, 103, 170, 250
political 35, 128, 139, 166, 200

portfolio	119, 220
portfolios	199, 240
portion	2
portray	65
positioned	183
positions	137
positive	81, 107, 111, 141
positively	204
possess	237
possible	49, 53, 67, 71, 85, 93, 125, 175, 198, 237
potential	52, 64, 84, 89, 107, 117, 127, 148, 174, 194, 238
practical	65, 76, 90, 93, 222
practice	160
practiced	132
practices	12, 80, 82, 91, 100, 102, 195, 217, 238, 249, 253
praise	235
precaution	3
precede	169
predict	134, 224
predicting	95
predictive	172
predictor	172
pre-filled	11
prepared	1, 258, 263
preparing	177, 207
present	97, 109-110, 136, 161, 180, 187, 238, 250
presented	1, 25, 223
presenting	234
preserve	44
preserved	73
pressing	131
pressures	136
prevalent	217
prevent	54, 257
preventive	210
previous	41, 190, 252, 255
previously	203, 225
priced	157
pricing	213
primary	51, 133
principles	138
priorities	46, 51, 55, 59
prioritize	193

priority 54, 57, 164, 235
probably   171
problem   18-19, 21-22, 25-28, 30, 32, 35, 41, 43, 48, 65, 222, 244-245, 247
problems   18-20, 23, 28, 79, 82, 99, 110, 139, 147, 191-192, 241
procedure   230, 258
procedures   12, 78, 94, 98, 100-101, 143, 157, 170, 187, 215, 217, 233, 245-246, 250, 257
proceed   206
proceeding   176
process   4-10, 12, 30, 32, 34, 37-39, 41, 55, 60-65, 67-75, 93-97, 100-103, 131-132, 137-138, 143, 145-147, 149, 151-154, 157, 161, 170, 174-175, 178, 191-192, 195, 202-203, 205-206, 212, 216, 219-220, 227, 231-232, 234-235, 238, 241, 247-248, 251, 254-255, 258, 261, 263
processed   257-258
processes   1, 53, 55, 61-64, 66-70, 72-74, 99, 102, 104, 132, 143, 154, 161, 203, 219-220, 223, 225, 229, 233, 241-242, 253, 255
procuring   219
produce   1, 170, 221, 231, 241
produced   63, 81, 263
produces   164
producing   149, 229
product   3, 57, 61, 63, 108, 114, 139-140, 151, 154, 167, 185, 189-190, 221-222, 226, 231-232, 247-248, 254, 261, 263
production   34, 79, 115, 233
products   3, 23, 26, 57, 114, 121, 139, 149, 173, 179, 219, 222, 225, 236
profits   185
program   19, 64, 95, 132, 136, 181, 241-242, 250
programme   219
programs   142, 199, 222, 240, 257
progress   33, 50, 84, 103, 109, 121, 139, 152, 158, 183, 191, 215, 230, 235, 241-242
project 4-6, 8-11, 22-23, 27-28, 44, 53, 60, 72, 87, 97-99, 106, 108, 115, 117, 119, 123-126, 128, 130-133, 135, 137-139, 141-146, 148-149, 151-156, 158, 160-163, 165-169, 171-181, 183-187, 190, 193-195, 197-199, 201-207, 211-212, 215-216, 219-226, 231, 236, 241-243, 247, 249, 252-256, 259, 261, 263-264
projected   194
projects   4, 46, 115, 120, 130, 132, 139, 142, 149, 151, 155, 177, 199, 201, 205, 207-208, 219, 221-222, 240, 247-248, 256

promising 114
promote 57, 74, 188
promptly 219, 236
proper 96, 145, 157
properly 37, 40, 131-132, 148, 158
property 230
Proposal 166, 214
proposals 103, 173
proposed 28, 49, 142, 148, 213-214, 251-252
protect 68, 113
protected 73
protection 119
protocols 189
proved 253
provide 19, 106, 109, 126, 135, 138, 141, 143, 147, 157-158, 177, 183, 235, 241, 244
provided 2, 14, 98, 153, 174, 180, 213, 264
provides 147
providing 96, 133, 135, 151, 166
provision 228
publisher 3
pulled 120
purchase 10, 211, 257-258
purchasing 1-2, 257
purpose 4, 12, 111, 171, 184, 192, 223, 228, 243
purposes 133
pursuing 2
pushing 119
qualified 39, 67, 71, 142
qualifies 64
qualify 61, 69
qualities 20
quality 6, 8, 12, 24, 52, 54, 62, 68-69, 74, 88, 95, 102, 116, 131, 139, 143-144, 151, 161, 174, 177-178, 180, 186-191, 196-197, 212-213, 219, 223, 229-230, 232
quantified 103
quarterly 246
question 13, 18, 30, 46, 60, 76, 93, 105, 128, 138, 234
questions 10-11, 13, 65, 176, 263
quickly 12, 68, 70
radically 63
ranking 207
rather 261

rating 213
rational 194
rationale 228
reached 27
reaching 112
reactivate 122
readiness 34, 160, 217
readings 96
realistic 27, 67, 112, 141, 207
Reality 202, 235
realize 2, 46
realized 115
realizing 1
really 10, 28, 41, 145
reason 106, 203
reasonable 89, 141, 144, 257
reasonably 157
reasons 33, 158
rebuild 114
receive 11-12, 32, 54, 263
received 33, 124, 235, 249
recently 107
recipient 22, 259
recognised 84
recognize 4, 18-21, 24-25, 78, 82, 235
recognized 19, 22, 24-26, 28, 63, 199, 236
recognizes 27
recommend 114, 120, 152
recording 3, 234
records 71, 122, 194, 259
recourse 258
recovery 55
recurring 157
redefine 27, 42
re-design 62
reduce 48, 59, 160, 204, 245
reduced 209
reducing 101, 108
references 265
reflect 95, 98, 104
reflection 101
reform 46, 103, 117, 121, 139
reforms 28, 49, 51

refreshed 2
refuses 209
regarding 118-119, 213-214, 222
region 136
Register 4, 7, 135, 203, 240
regret 77
regular 33, 38, 63, 251
regularly 44, 185, 241
regulation 238, 257-258
regulatory 28, 231
relate 67, 225
related 23, 50, 68, 99, 132, 187, 199, 240, 245, 247, 264
relating 185
relation 20, 24, 85, 111, 229
relations 105
relative 103, 235
relatively 115
release 190, 199, 212
released 224
releases 251
Relevance 257
relevant 32, 49, 97, 185, 195, 216, 231
reliable 210
relieved 2
relocation 141
remain 263
remaining 183, 262
remember 175
remunerate 87
repair 198
repeatable 205
rephrased 12
replace 53
replaced 138
replanning 157
replicated 255
Report 8, 84, 96, 189, 221, 230-231, 243, 251
reported 161, 193, 247
reporting 66, 97, 110, 157, 190, 193, 203, 215
reports 2, 54, 98, 135, 182, 197, 202
repository 143, 197, 212, 264
represent 83, 225-226
reproduced 3

reputation 115
request 8, 65, 185, 214, 223-226
requested 3, 79, 214, 226
requests 223-224, 258
require 38, 53, 66-67, 102, 104, 170, 238, 258, 263
required 23, 31, 34, 36, 39, 49, 66, 71, 86, 90-91, 95, 138, 145, 147, 153, 162-164, 168, 174, 189, 196-197, 230, 241, 249, 261
requiring 135, 259
research 23, 114, 152, 173-174, 233, 238, 262
resemble 220
reserve 157
reserved 3
reserves 194
reside 82, 212
Resistance 217
resolution 199, 233
resolve 20, 23, 27, 232
resolved 219, 233, 239
resource 6-7, 115, 157, 160, 170-172, 174, 180, 197-198, 221
resources 2, 4, 10, 18, 22, 25, 32, 43, 55, 70, 86, 94-95, 101, 108, 115-116, 136, 141, 146-147, 151, 153, 160, 162, 165, 168-169, 180, 183, 231, 239, 241, 244, 246, 261
respect 3
respond 139
responded 14
responding 204
response 19, 23, 94, 97-99, 101, 173, 251
responses 77, 111, 207
responsive 176, 184
result 81, 83, 139, 151, 159, 184, 226, 243, 259, 261
resulted 100
resulting 68, 157
results 11, 32, 36, 61, 76, 78, 80, 83-85, 90, 97-98, 138, 164, 184, 219-220, 229, 238, 241, 253
Retain 105
retained 66
retention 48
retrospect 120
return 81, 116, 168, 187
returns 189
revenue 18, 55
revenues 51
review 12, 34, 72, 177, 180-181, 189, 216, 229, 233, 263

reviewed 39, 152, 212
Reviewer 236-237
reviewers 235
reviews 151, 197, 215, 249
revised 63, 100
revisions 259
reward 57-58, 222
rewarded 28
rewards 102
rework 51, 57
rights 3
robustness 166
roll-out 217
routine 94, 246
routinely 193
rundown 180
rushing 199
safety 114
sample 187
satisfied 114, 145, 182, 231, 253-254, 261
satisfies 248
satisfy 132
satisfying 114
savings 34, 46, 52, 63
scalable 78
scenario 36, 41
scenes 2
schedule 5-6, 35, 52, 94, 126, 139, 160, 168, 177-178, 180, 186, 203, 223, 225, 231, 251, 255
scheduled 144, 146, 158, 198, 214, 241, 245
Schedules 168, 214
scheduling 158, 160
scheme 101
Science 64, 175
scientific 175
Scorecard 4, 14-16, 219
scorecards 102
Scores 16
scoring 12
screen 233
scripts 153
seamless 117
second 14

secret 2
secrets 1
section 14, 28-29, 44-45, 59, 75, 91, 104, 129
sector 247
securing   56, 116
security   19, 62, 90, 104, 135, 154, 189, 226, 261
segmented   37
segments   39, 129
select 69, 103
selected   80, 183, 217, 246
selecting   67, 107
Selection   7, 213, 215
selects 238
self-help   2
sellers 3, 173
selling 124
senior 104, 108, 110, 127
sensitive   39, 52, 139
sequencing   121, 198, 219
series 13
Service 1-4, 10, 57, 81, 87, 95, 114, 151, 167, 185, 221-222, 263
services   3, 38, 50, 57, 106, 121, 128, 213, 219-220, 245, 251, 254, 258-259
session 158
setbacks   70
setting 112, 123
several 74
severely   62
shared 69, 94, 184, 227, 245
sharing 85, 101, 188, 233
shifts 26
shopping   1
shortly 258
should 10, 20, 22, 25-26, 35, 38, 41, 52, 54, 59, 64, 66, 69, 71, 74, 80, 89-90, 99, 106, 109, 112, 115, 122, 126, 135, 139-140, 143, 145-146, 151, 163, 173-174, 176, 186, 201, 203-204, 206-207, 213-214, 219, 232, 238, 241, 263
signature   111
signatures   170
signed 151-152
signers 259
similar 41, 44, 61, 65, 81, 136, 163-164, 174, 189-190, 194, 205
simple 115, 193, 243, 247

Simply 11
single 119
single-use 10
situation 2, 23, 46, 132, 178, 245, 247
situations 100
skeptical 123
skills 19-20, 64, 108, 116-117, 166, 196, 212, 235-236, 243, 264
smallest 27, 81
soccer 1
social 123, 210
societal 120
software 23, 132, 140, 146, 154, 173, 177, 179, 201, 205, 219, 224, 249, 251
solicit 33
soliciting 234
solution 1, 58, 65, 76, 78, 80, 84, 89-90, 93, 153, 251-252
solutions 53, 87, 89, 100, 142
solved 26
solving 244
Someone 10
someones 236
something 113, 151, 194
Sometimes 53
source 7, 117, 119, 210, 213
sources 34, 65-66, 207
special 31, 98
specific 11, 21, 32, 34, 42, 64, 132, 144, 162, 165-166, 168, 170-171, 173, 179, 195, 206, 216, 221, 225, 235, 256
specified 112, 157, 193, 209
specify 236
spending 2, 144
spoken 107
sponsor 19, 134, 254
sponsors 19, 192, 241
spread 95, 101
stability 189
staffed 43
staffing 19, 102, 160
standard 10, 95, 97, 132, 160, 170, 173, 189, 251
standards 12-13, 96, 100, 103, 131, 153-154, 191, 225, 229, 238
started 11, 166, 168
starting 12, 139

start-up 231
stated 107, 123, 148, 160, 187, 257, 264
statement 5, 13, 79, 82, 151, 158, 211, 216
statements 14, 29, 32, 35, 45, 59, 75, 91, 104, 129, 229-230
static 224
statistics 179
status 8, 75, 131, 158, 212, 221, 231, 247, 251
statute 238
statutory 231
steady 51
steering 187, 212
storage 223
stories 43
strategic 78, 81, 103, 128, 187, 197, 249
strategies 86, 108, 117, 152, 205, 227-228
strategy 23, 52, 84, 87, 97, 113, 116, 119, 126, 153, 160, 199, 220
Stream 66, 72
strengths 154, 166, 234, 253
stretch 123
strive 123, 219
Strongly 13, 18, 30, 46, 60, 76, 93, 105
structure 5-6, 49, 87, 115, 120, 139, 155, 171, 218, 230
structured 110, 161, 214
structures 244
stupid 126
styles 187
subject 11-12, 32, 145
submitted 225
submitting 189
subsequent 160
subset 27
sub-teams 237
subtotals 181
succeed 47, 127
success 21, 37-38, 40-41, 43, 47-48, 50, 81, 85-86, 89, 94, 108, 114, 116, 119, 124, 126, 131, 134, 153, 180-181, 198, 222, 227, 236, 238
successes 117
successful 1, 66, 86, 99, 105, 125-126, 171, 199, 221, 239
succession 103
suddenly 205
suffered 235

sufficient   237, 263-264
suggest   207, 224
suggested   99, 225-226
suitable   232
Sunday   1
superior   1, 197
supervisor   234
supplier   82, 111
suppliers   38, 63, 65, 127, 230, 258
supplies   179, 254, 258
supply 51, 166
support   3, 10, 18, 60, 65, 96, 99-100, 106, 108, 133, 147, 170, 187, 201, 218, 251
supported   69, 138
supporting   80, 90, 96, 215
supportive   196
supports   132
supposed   229
surface   99
SUSTAIN   4, 91, 105
Sustaining   94, 166
symptom   18, 50
system 12, 43, 65, 67, 99, 111, 127, 147-148, 154, 157-158, 171, 173, 193, 224, 226, 229-230, 238, 245, 247-248
systematic   55
systems   1, 61-62, 67, 70, 88-89, 102, 213, 215, 247, 253
tackle 50
tactical   78
tactics 227
tailored   2
takers 152
taking 55, 201, 221, 234
talent 71, 110
talents 108
talking 10
target 39, 127, 180
targets 123, 182, 248
tariffs 257
tasked 93
teaching   230
teaming   233
teamwork   79
technical   60, 83, 136, 147, 158, 167, 205, 213

techniques 117, 215
technology 1, 53, 86, 95, 114, 139, 167, 201-202, 206, 233
templates 10-11
testable 30
test-cycle 191
tested 131
testing 148, 189-190, 249-250
thematic 137
themselves 1, 127, 243
theory 98
therefore 210
therein 193
things 85, 125, 131, 181, 190, 194, 211
thinking 81, 129
thorough 82, 186
thought 234
threat 24
threaten 177
threats 1-2
through 63, 74, 78, 127, 228
throughout 3, 109, 174
throughput 174
Thursday 1
tighter 123
time-bound 32
timeframe 62, 165, 183
timeframes 23
timeline 154, 225, 241
timely 25, 82, 194, 211, 223, 231, 233, 257, 264
Timescales 136
timetable 257
timing 258
together 114
tolerable 143
tolerances 84
tolerated 175
tomorrow 104, 131
toolkit 1-2
toolkits 1-2
top-down 97
topics 83
toward 101, 221
towards 2, 136, 139, 144

traced 153
tracked 198
tracking 44, 103, 152
traction 123
trade-in 257
trademark 3
trademarks 3
tradeoff 213
trade-offs 161
trained 40, 187, 213
training 22, 28, 66, 71, 84, 98, 101-102, 217, 222, 233, 237, 249, 264
trainings 23
Transfer 14, 29, 45, 59, 75, 92-93, 102, 104, 129, 251
transfers 257
transition 127, 207
translated 34
trending 215
trends 61, 63-64, 83, 114, 141, 187, 189, 210
trigger 76, 84
triggers 89, 144
trophy 109
trouble 122
trying 10, 119, 128, 134, 190, 209
turnaround 165
ultimate 110
unaware 1
unbiased 249
unclear 34
uncovered 2
underlying 90
undermine 128
understand 35, 64, 145, 177, 205, 207, 235
understood 88-89, 124, 148, 206, 243, 250
undertake 70, 204
underway 79
unique 2, 109, 233, 250
Unless 10
unplanned 233
unprepared 1
unresolved 161, 170
update 1
Updated 11-12, 211

updates 12, 102, 251
upfront 217
usability 86, 127
useful 80, 102, 155, 202, 263
usefully 12, 27
usually 1, 257
utilised 215
utility 175
utilized 238
utilizing 1
validate 54, 247
validated 30, 39, 41, 68, 75
Validation 247
Validity 147
valuable 10
values 104, 127, 195, 210, 230
variables 103, 174, 227
variance 8, 158, 193, 235-236, 245-246
variances 143, 161, 173, 245
variants 258
variation 18, 36, 65-66, 101
variety 86
vendor 82, 197, 211
vendors 26, 67, 151, 197
verified 12, 30, 39, 41, 75
verify 48-50, 52-57, 97, 104, 152, 223, 248, 260
verifying 151
version 251, 265
versions 37-38
versus 146
vested 122
viable 100, 156
vision 127, 141, 230
visits 197
visualize 162, 175
voices 135
volatile 82
volunteers 250
waited 2
walking 2
warrant 232
warranty 3, 189
weaknesses 136, 186, 213, 253

weather 136
weeknights 1
wellbeing 187
whether 10, 98, 107, 196, 238, 258
-which 199, 206
widespread 95
widgets 185
willing 185, 208, 249
window 165
win-win 245
withheld 257
within 1-2, 70, 89, 157, 165, 176, 179, 193, 210, 216, 221, 225, 234, 254, 257
without1, 3, 14, 114, 126, 139, 148, 206, 214, 225, 258-259
worked 154, 194, 250, 256
workers 107
workflow 73, 228
workforce 19, 83, 114, 127, 129, 197
working 2, 98, 153, 194-195, 202, 207
work-life 196
workload 201
Worksheet 6, 175, 183
worst-case 41
writing 145, 149, 187
written 3, 187, 230
youhave 158, 178
yourself 112, 119, 127

Manufactured by Amazon.ca
Acheson, AB

Does the board have assurance that the information is accurate and complete?

This Collaborative Decision Making Guide is unlike books you're used to. If you're looking for a textbook, this might not be for you. This book and its included digital components is for you who understands the importance of asking great questions. This gives you the questions to uncover the Collaborative Decision Making challenges you're facing and generate better solutions to solve those problems. Defining, designing, creating, and implementing a process to solve a challenge or meet an objective is the most valuable role... In EVERY group, company, organization and department.

Unless you're talking a one-time, single-use project, there should be a process. That process needs to be designed by someone with a complex enough perspective to ask the right questions. Someone capable of asking the right questions and step back and say, 'What are we really trying to accomplish here? And is there a different way to look at it?'

This Self-Assessment empowers people to do just that - whether their title is entrepreneur, manager, consultant, (Vice-)President, CxO etc... - they are the people who rule the future. They are the person who asks the right questions to make Collaborative Decision Making investments work better.

This Collaborative Decision Making All-Inclusive Self-Assessment enables You to be that person.

INCLUDES all the tools you need to an in-depth Collaborative Decision Making Self-Assessment. Featuring new and updated case-based questions, organized into seven core levels of Collaborative Decision Making maturity, this Self-Assessment will help you identify areas in which Collaborative Decision Making improvements can be made.

ISBN 9780655316084